International Misadventures with the aid of a Fly Rod

David M. Schultz

THE AUTHOR

David M. (Dave) Schultz is a retired fisheries biologist and environmental engineer with degrees in Biology (B.S.) and Engineering Science (M.S.) from the University of California Berkeley. He currently lives in Newport Beach, California with his wife Mary and two sons Michael and Adam. When not at home tying flies, researching his next journey or surfing, he is usually traveling and fly fishing, often at his restored fly fishing lodge on the banks of Fall River in Central Oregon.

ACKNOWLEDGEMENTS

I've been blessed with good guidance from family, teachers and friends throughout my life, even if I didn't (and don't) always listen.

Thanks to my parents. You knew that all children need to discover a passion that stimulates their curiosity, enthusiasm for life, and desire to learn. Thanks to my wife Mary and sons Adam and Michael for supporting my adventures and often joining me. Special thanks to Mary for her many hours of fine editing; as critical as my dreaded high school English teacher but, thankfully, only when she has that red pen and clipboard in her hands.

Thanks to my fly fishing and adventure buddies. Some of you are in the pages of these stories and others are in photos and memories not yet put on paper: Mike Marello, Steve Bredehoft, Jeff Jurach, Kirk Macintosh, Rob Gillanders, Paul Burton, Stephanie Hagar, Kirk von Meeteren, Len Vanderstar and Dave Slavensky. I hope to join you all on many more great adventures to come.

Cover design and graphics by Mary Schultz

"Time is like a river. You cannot touch the same water twice because the flow that has passed will never pass again. Find your passion, take risks, seek adventure, and get the most from every day of your life."

(multiple authors)

CONTENTS

INTRODUCTION

At the age of seven, I snuck out of the house and walked to our local creek. I found a paper cup and tried to catch some minnows that were darting around in the shallow current. They were too quick but I was able to catch a few tiny tadpoles in the slower water. It was quite an adventure and four things happened as a result:

1. My mom and dad grounded me for two weeks, and that included no ice cream.
2. My parents, both school teachers, let me keep the tadpoles alive in my small kiddie wading pool in our backyard. They bought fish food for them and told me they weren't actually fish. When they became frogs we took them back to the creek and let them go.
3. I was determined to go back and catch those minnows.
4. My dad took me to his friend's sporting goods store and bought spin casting rods for the two of us.

My love of the outdoors was no secret to my parents. They took our family on camping trips to Sierra Nevada lakes and streams at every opportunity. At the age of ten I rode in the family station wagon from California to Yellowstone National Park for the first time. The geysers, hot springs, bears and bison were fascinating, but most unforgettable to me were the fly anglers at Fishing Bridge and Buffalo Ford. I was mesmerized by the waving rods and the random dimples as trout rose on the Yellowstone River. I earned my first fly rod, mowing lawns and pulling weeds, a few months later. I have not wandered far from a fly rod since.

When I'm asked why fly fishing is so popular, my typical short response is, "Because it's fun." On occasion, I attempt a more thoughtful and detailed answer. Here's a list:

•*Fly fishing takes us to some of the world's most beautiful wild places with the people we'd most like to be with.*
•*Fly fishing blends art, science, sport and tradition.*
•*Multiple levels of skill are involved and there is great satisfaction in the lifelong challenge of improving on those skills.*
•*For the curious like me, fly fishing allows the angler to probe deep into the mysteries hidden beneath the water's surface.*
•*It encourages respect for the natural environment. Fly anglers are often staunch conservationists working to preserve and rehabilitate natural habitats.*
•*Successful fly fishing requires a high level of focus and concentration that pushes life's anxieties to the back of our thoughts during time spent on the water.*
•*Fly fishing takes us on adventures, and often surprising misadventures, that challenge us physically and mentally.*
•*It allows us to compress some of life's best moments into a shorter time frame.*
•*Fly anglers experience the peace and tranquility of flowing water away from the city.*
•*Successful fly fishing encourages physical fitness and a healthy life style.*
•*Fly anglers can experience the challenge and excite-*

ment of a hunt without killing their prey. We are able to release our catch alive.
•Successful fly anglers are keen observers, a good trait for getting the most out of any adventure as well as life itself.
•Fly fishing is fun!

The art and science of fly fishing can take years to master; casting, reading water, fly selection and presentation, and fly tying. The truth is that fly fishing is never fully mastered and that is part of the allure.

All of us who enjoy fly fishing have a passion for travel, adventure and the outdoors. A fly rod in its most basic form is merely a tool to make a more intimate connection with nature. For some people, a walk along the riverbank is enough, but a fly rod allows the angler a more thorough examination and deeper understanding of the natural world.

There are many tools that can lead to adventure; a kayak, skis, surfboard, scuba gear, climbing rope, mountain bike, river raft, sailboat and more. Each requires practice and dedication, focus and concentration. The result is a more personal and profound wilderness experience. I've tried many of those tools and most often choose the fly rod for its versatility and its blend of art with science. It can be used anywhere that water is found, always beckoning its owner to spectacular new locations and new adventures.

Human beings did not evolve on crowded freeways, in shopping malls or while scanning the Internet on smartphones. So it seems only natural that many of us will take any opportunity we can to escape the city and head out to wilder environments. That might imply that fly anglers are lower on the evolutionary tree, but the success of most fly fishers in today's urban environment does not support the hypothesis.

Like many of you, I am preparing for my next fly fishing journey, and the one after that, nearly every day of the year. My cluttered fly tying desk is always calling and I am constantly arranging and rearranging my gear while reading magazine and Internet articles about possible new fly fishing frontiers and journeys, while reminiscing about the old. Come along and join me on a few adventures and the unexpected misadventures that go hand-in-hand. We'll be like seven-year-olds chasing minnows.

1 CUTTHROAT & GRIZZLIES

A Frightening Encounter

Yellowstone National Park

While we were in our twenties, my good friend Jeff and I went on many long backpacking and fly fishing road trips from our homes in California. Everything was done on a tight budget. In those days my money was spread pretty thin on things almost as important as fly fishing, like food. Jeff was not the fly fishing fanatic that I was but he loved our wilderness adventures (Jeff later became a skilled rock climber and has scaled all of the big walls in Yosemite).

Back then my most important fishing tools were an old Datsun pickup truck, a Kelty Tioga backpack that was my high school graduation gift, and my handmade five-piece fly rod.

I built the pack rod from an eight-foot 5-wt. Lamiglas fly rod blank while I was a senior in high school. I cut up my first fly rod, a beat and broken Wright and McGill, to make light fiberglass ferrules for my new pack rod, the fly rod equivalent of an organ transplant. It was a tedious task of sliding pieces of the older blank over the new blank until the inner and outer sections fit snuggly together. Then I marked and cut short pieces of the outer blank that became the ferrules. The guides were wrapped with great care and the cork rings were glued and sanded to a smooth even finish. I took a lot of pride in that rod and still fish with it occasionally today, many years later.

Jeff and I made the 22-hour drive to Yellowstone National Park quite a few times. It was my favorite fly fishing destination and remains high on my list today. In those days we figured we could drive non-stop to anywhere as long as the rotating passenger got a little sleep. My cassette tape "boom box" sat between us on the bench seat and kept the driver company when the passenger nodded off. Finding 24-hour gas stations could be a problem. The bright neon "Terrible Herbst" service station sign standing tall above Lovelock, Nevada at 3 AM was always a welcome sight.

My rusty red Datsun (the company now known as Nissan) was fairly reliable but had a few quirky personality traits. The alternator, for example, would occasionally freeze up on the highway. The driver would be alerted by the small red dashboard light or, if he missed that, by the smell of the burning fan belt a few minutes later. It was a simple task to pull over, leave the engine running, open the hood, and give the static alternator a whack with the plastic mallet I carried under the seat. That would get the machinery spinning again. A new alternator was about the same price as a fly rod and reel so I kept that part (barely) working for years.

That old red truck was my Harley Davidson. It symbolized freedom on the open road; freedom, if only for a few weeks at a time, from life's responsibilities and concerns. As a bonus, it had space in the pickup bed for a few backpacks, fly rod cases and other outdoor gear that wouldn't fit on a motorcycle.

Yellowstone was, as it remains today, an amazing place to visit; the world's greatest concentration of natural wonders. The geo-thermal features are otherworldly, the waterfalls stunning, and the big mammals; elk, bison, moose, sheep, pronghorn and bears an awesome symbol of wilderness left nearly untouched for hundreds of years. My main reason for returning to Yellowstone so many times was, however, the fly fishing.

Back then you didn't need a license to fish Yellowstone. That saved a few dollars. To save a few more we would sometimes avoid even the minimal campground fees and sleep along the park's roadway pullouts. Early one morning I was interrupted from a deep sleep by the loud bang of a car door slamming shut. Jeff and I were camped out under the stars in the "free" forest only 100 feet or so from the road. I pretended to remain asleep as I heard heavy footsteps moving towards us through the low brush. When the walking stopped only a few feet away, I glanced through the slits of my nearly-closed eyes to the sight of two tall leather boots towering above my face. "Morn'n boys", said the National Park Ranger in his deep raspy voice. "If you're out of here in five minutes, I won't have to write you up."

You've never seen a campsite cleaned up and abandoned so quickly! Our ranger friend crossed his arms and glowered at us under his wide-brimmed Smokey-the-Bear hat, but I'm pretty sure he was struggling to hold back his laughter. Today you can't get away with sleeping outside of designated camping areas in Yellowstone; too many visitors are stressing the Park's resources.

Our main destination on this particular trip was the upper Lamar River. We wanted to explore the smaller more remote water above the vast Lamar Valley that is well known for its herds of huge bison and big Yellowstone cutthroat trout.

After a quick visit to the Old Faithful Geyser, reliable as always, we stopped by the ranger station to pick up our mandatory but free backcountry permit. Our plan was to park at the confluence of the Lamar and Soda Butte Creek, work our way fly fishing and camping up the Lamar to the headwaters, hike over the divide at Pelican Cone, and then fish down Pelican Creek to the access road near Yellowstone Lake. The ranger made it clear to us; this was a long journey through prime grizzly country that was not often visited by humans. That sounded perfect to a couple of 23-year olds looking for a good wilderness adventure. I'd be lying though if I didn't admit that backpacking through wild grizzly country, with no protection other than our wits and fate, sparked some ominous thoughts. As a kid I had watched those National Geographic specials where the Craighead Brothers studied Yellowstone grizzlies. I remember how a big angry male had torn up their station wagon. I was not completely naive.

We stocked up with enough food for eight days on the trail with an emphasis on Kraft Mac & Cheese, a few cans of mixed nuts, raisins, dried apricots, Gouda cheese, oatmeal and a small frying pan to cook up the trout that we expected to be plentiful.

I parked the old pickup near the head of the big Lamar Valley and we took one final inventory of our gear. Worn running shoes served as wet wading boots and they came in handy immediately as we crossed frigid Soda Butte Creek. Dry socks and hiking boots came out of our backpacks on the far bank and we headed into the upper Lamar Valley. We would not see another human for a week.

The faint trail became even more sinuous and indistinct as we moved upstream. It was apparently used more by the local wildlife then by hikers. The sub-alpine environment was a combination of dense pine forest and swampy wildflower-filled meadows with a few small aspen groves; perfect grizzly habitat. Above us in the distance were the ridgelines and peaks that defined the Lamar River drainage. Some snowfields and cornices still lingered on the high mountains and passes.

As we moved up the small river, I tended to linger, looking for trout, while Jeff explored up ahead. Alone in grizzly country, the spectacular wilderness inspired a sense of freedom and serenity, but with underlying traces of loneliness and fear. I became extra sensitive to the environment, almost as if I was becoming part of the wilderness around me. The sounds of birds chirping, water gurgling and wind whooshing were amplified over softer, and possibly imagined, snaps, clicks and thumps. I scanned the brush and hillsides ahead and occasionally turned to inspect the ground I had just traveled. I often felt that I was being watched from behind.

I stopped at any likely looking water and rigged up my fly rod. Often it would remain set up for most of the day and my dry hiking boots would stay in the backpack. My Yellowstone fly selection was simple in those days comprised mainly of dry flies that I had tied; Adams, elk hair caddis, a few fast water Humpys and a simple grizzly hackle and peacock body pattern, most in sizes #14 and #16. I added a few hare's ear and pheasant tail nymphs and that was it. That was all you needed. With their short growing season, untouched Yellowstone cutthroat trout are often ravenous. Amazingly, they can grow to good size even in small streams; eighteen-to-twenty inches and even larger. With their yellow-gold flanks, black spots and bright orange gill slashes, the Yellowstone cutthroat is a worthy aquatic mascot for the wildest places on the eastern slope of the Northern Rocky Mountains.

We set up our small tent each afternoon near a larger pool in the river. Evening caddis hatches would often result in a flurry of rises. It was an easy task for us to catch a few trout for dinner. I would continue fishing and release the others while Jeff took care of other tasks. This was before catch-and-release fly fishing had gained popularity. C&R wasn't so much a conscious conservation effort back then. It was a way to continue fishing when you wanted to catch more trout than you wanted to kill. Three or four were all we ever needed for dinner. The rest were carefully released back to the water. I suspect that my attitude was similar to many other fly anglers during this transition period to C&R; a fish was more valuable in the stream than in the frying pan.

We caught trout as close as a rod's length from our feet. It was so simple. After several evenings of big hatches and easy dry fly fishing, Jeff made a proclamation that I'll never forget, "This fly fishing can get a little boring".

Ha! Blasphemy! How many times have I thought back to that statement during a difficult fishing day? But that was Yellowstone fly fishing back then.

The days passed and, despite our high level of awareness, we did not spot any bears; just deer and a few elk. Maybe it was our intentional loud conversations and off-key singing as we approached dense vegetation. That may have allowed any bears in the area to quietly escape our attention. We saw no grizzlies nor their hated cousins the black bear. We did see signs however; tracks in the meadow mud, scat and apparent bear fur on "scratching trees". The bark on a few pine trees had been cut in neat vertical rows; bear claws. We knew that bears were near. At night the sounds of lightly rushing river water usually lulled me to sleep. At other times I lay in my sleeping bag and imagined faint and haunting overtones within the gurgling of the flow; men talking, a baby crying and bears grunting.

By the fifth day the Lamar was a mere brook as we had crossed many of the main tributaries. Pelican Cone, above the tree line and with some late-season snow, loomed a few miles ahead. We soon reached the divide separating the Lamar and Pelican Creek watersheds. The view from the ridgeline was remarkable with the jagged Absaroka-Beartooth Mountains to the north and the deep blue alpine ocean of Yellowstone Lake to our south. We bid farewell to the Lamar and hiked down to the Pelican Creek Valley.

Pelican Creek was, and is today, even better known as prime grizzly habitat than the Lamar. The wide meandering creek is a major spawning stream for big cutthroat from Yellowstone Lake and the grizzlies have known about this seasonal feast for centuries. We had fly fished there on a previous backpacking trip with good success.

I saw no sign of spawning trout but some large Yellowstone Lake cutthroat remained in the clear flow winding through the meadow. While carefully walking through the dry meadow grass along the stream bank, I spotted two big fish lying near the undercut on the far bank 30-feet away. My first cast, across and slightly upstream, flew a bit long and the brown elk hair caddis hung up in the grass on the opposite side. The trout were oblivious to my tight leader suspended in the air a few feet above as I gently tugged to free the fly. Then with a tiny "pip" my caddis came free and landed just upstream of the two trout.

The larger cutty spotted it immediately and began to rise towards my imitation, its body angled steeply upward. The rise was slow and deliberate, one inch upward for every three inches the trout backed down the mild current. The big cutthroat stalled its ascent just below my fly and, with fins waving, drifted down current another few feet. I squinted hard and my rod wrist quivered. Then the fish kissed my caddis and was on! The trout flashed across the wide run several times before it tired and I was able to lead it into shallow water near my feet. It was a beauty, nearly twenty-inches long! I gently released the fish, replaced my drenched fly and moved quietly downstream searching for the next.

Further down Pelican Creek and late in the day, Jeff and I came upon an old unoccupied ranger's cabin in the forest edge near the meadow. For some reason this area felt extremely bearish, perhaps because of its proximity to the bottom of the meadow where the dark forest pressed closest to the creek. We checked out the heavy weathered log cabin to see if we could enter. The thick timber door was locked tight. The window was covered by vertical wooden planks held in place by two rusted steel bars. The horizontal bars, bolted on each side of the sturdy timber window frame, were strong but slightly loose against the planks. Noted.

We set up our tent near the ranger cabin and began cooking dinner on our little brass Svea stove as the day's light faded. The sun had fallen behind the hills about ten minutes earlier. Then, just as our beef stroganoff noodles began to boil, it happened. Two massive mounds of fur lumbered out of the forest and into the meadow just a few hundred feet from our tent. Grizzlies! Damn!

19

Our hunger disappeared immediately replaced by the rush of adrenaline. Jeff shut off the stove and, without saying a word, we both ran to the cabin's iron window bars. With four boots on the heavy wooden windowsill and four hands on the lower bar, we pulled with all our strength. The bar bent back towards us a few inches! The upper bar followed and also bowed out slightly as we strained against it. We struggled with the window cover slats and slid the first one out from between the bars. There was no glass. Within a few minutes we had the boards out and there was enough space between the bars to wriggle through. We threw our sleeping bags in along with our water bottles, headlamps and a few snacks.

The interior of the cabin was organized but it did not appear to have been used for some time. Thin dusty mattresses hung from the log rafters and we pulled them down to the floor. The heavy timbers separating us from the bears outside, along with the mattresses, should have insured a good night's sleep. As it turned out though, we both had a restless night interrupted by strange dreams. There was a big double-bladed axe hanging on the inside cabin wall. Both Jeff and I dreamt of huge furry knife-tipped paws reaching through the steel bars while we swung the axe. Crazy!

The next morning was bright and windless. We crawled out between the iron bars for a quick recon and bathroom break. There was no sign of the bears. We climbed back into the cabin and rehung the mattresses. The cabin interior could have used a good dusting but we were more interested in getting back out on the river. We replaced the window slats and worked our way downstream towards Yellowstone Lake.

This was our last day on the trail and we arrived at the road by midafternoon. We laid our backpacks down just off the roadway and stuck our thumbs out, hoping for a ride. Within 30 minutes or so an old van pulled over. It turned out to be an elderly couple from Michigan that had built their dream RV from an old milk truck. We were separated by more than a generation but both on the similar journeys. Our loud conversation over the engine noise made the long drive back to my truck pass quickly. We gave our sincere thanks, threw our backpacks into the pickup bed and were back on the road. Jeff and I promised each other to return soon to this natural wonderland of trout, multi-colored hot springs, geysers, waterfalls, bison and bears.

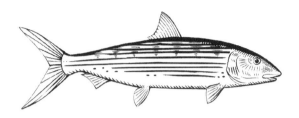

2 MISADVENTURES IN BELIZE

Bonefish and Bull Sharks and Crocs Oh My!

The tropical jungles and mangrove coastline resisted human encroachment for 3,000 years before it was named Belize. From ancient Mayans to modern developers, human expansion has battled nature while hurricanes, torrential rains, and ever-encroaching rainforest growth have fought to reclaim it back.

After years of planning and daydreaming, my long-time fly fishing buddy Mike and I took our first ever bonefishing trip to Turneffe Island in Belize. This was many years ago, but vivid memories of our tropical adventure remain. We cast to bonefish on the ankle-deep barrier reef while watching huge iridescent green parrotfish cruise with their backs half out of the water. We waded the calm mangrove edges on the inside and cast to more bonefish. We snorkeled the warm blue tidal passes over pure white sand. Brown bus-sized coral heads sprinkled with brightly colored tropical fish sprung up here and there while five-foot-long barracuda patrolled nearby. We searched the tiny tropical island of Turneffe for 2,000-year-old pottery fragments from the ancient Mayans and found some!

The food was fantastic and included all the freshly caught lobster and fish we could eat along with the local Belikin beer. We were careful to follow the winding marked pathways over the white sand from our elevated beach bungalow to the dining room. Hundreds of pink and white conch shells delineated the "safe zone" where falling coconuts from the swaying palms above were less likely to impact the head of an unsuspecting visitor.

We quickly became friends with our guide Alberto, a young Belizean local who already had years of guiding and boating experience. Mike and I are like kids on Christmas morning while we're fishing and Alberto soon loosened up and joined in the fun. We were rank bonefish amateurs standing on the bow of Alberto's flats boat and casting to cruising fish. "Bonefeesh at 2 o'clock, 40 feet!" exclaimed Alberto in an excited whisper. "Shoot it out mon!"

I frantically made a few false casts and sent my fly out in the general vicinity of the silver ghost that was plainly visible to Alberto, but invisible to me. "No mon, you cost behind da feesh".

Ten minutes later Alberto called out another and this time I saw it too. "No mon, you cost too close to da feesh....spook!"

We blew many attempts at intercepting the moving bonefish but usually had another opportunity within a few minutes. We started to have a little success with a couple of bonefish hooked up on flies that we had tied during the many months of anticipation before the trip.

We all hooted when a hooked fish shot across the sparkling tropical sand flats like a tiny silver torpedo. The drag on my old Martin reel moaned and screamed. "Your reel is bery sick mon" mentioned Alberto on several occasions. Fortunately it worked slightly better than it sounded.

We had so much fun with all of this, in a spectacular tropical setting no less, that we decided to make a little bonefishing comedy clip with the video camera that I had brought along. As the cameraman, I laid on my back on the bottom of the flats skiff with Mike on the bow and Alberto up on the poling platform. We had read about some inexperienced fly casters and their agitated tarpon guides in Florida and did our best to recreate the scene.

Alberto rehearsed his lines. Then......"Annoyed Fly Fishing Guide take one. Aaaaand action!"

"Bonefeesh at 50 feet coming right at you! Twelve o'clock! Geet et out dere queek mon!.....No mon, you make a bod cost, a bery bod cost".

The final film cut was pretty good but the picture shook a little at the end of the scene; it was me, the cameraman, trying to hold back my laughter.

The week at Turneffe blew by like the warm eastern trade winds and we were soon on our last day at the lodge. Other than a brief run into Guatemala and tour of the Mayan ruins at Altun Ha, we had four more largely unplanned days left in Belize and discussed our options with our new friend Alberto. "I have two days off mon. Come to my house near Belize City an I will take you to feesh and explore da Sibun River".

Yes! Great plan Alberto!

We met the following morning, not at Alberto's home but at a dockside restaurant along the sweltering Belize City waterfront. Dozens of wooden shacks and slightly more substantial metal-sided old buildings sat tentatively on barnacle-encrusted pilings above the brown water. Boats of all sizes, colors and various states of disrepair puttered around the harbor. It could have been a movie set for any number of locations; old Shanghai, Jamaica, the Amazon, Vietnam or the Philippines. The scent of partially burned diesel fuel, fried fish and a hint of raw sewage filled the sticky air.

We expected Alberto to pull up to the docks in one of the lodge's flats skiffs. Instead we heard our names called from out over the water and watched as Alberto motored over in an old partially-covered wooden transport vessel of about twenty feet in length. He waved us aboard and we hopped on. Alberto had brought a guest along, his six-year-old son Alberto Jr. Young Alberto was pretty quiet, but when he did speak it was in a clicky English dialect not familiar to us.

We headed out into the bay and towards the mouth of the Sibun River in the bright tropical sun. The rickety shacks and crisscrossing boat traffic gave way to a more tranquil scene of mangroves and palm trees. Within a few miles, the channel narrowed as thick jungle vegetation closed in on us from the riverbanks. The current was swirling and flowing upstream from the bay; a rising tide. This was not the pure tropical water we had experienced out on Turneffe Island with hundred-foot visibility. We could barely see a few feet into this tea-stained soup.

We paused for a few minutes to drift and cast our flies towards the jungle edges. A yellow and black toucan with a lime green beak flashed through the tall trees just behind the mangroves and a resident Howler monkey chattered a warning. "Dis is not for sweeming mon", explained Alberto during a break. "Da currents are strong and da BEEG crocks and bull sharks live here!"

We didn't doubt that at all.

The tall rainforest growth along the river channel kept us mainly in the shade now, but the lack of a cool ocean breeze was stifling. We reeled in our lines. Alberto accelerated further up river and the increased air movement was welcomed. His destination was a deep cenote spring along the river that apparently held huge tarpon.

There was little sign of civilization but we did see a local fisherman waving to us from the muddy riverbank. He pulled on a slimy old rope and dragged a twenty-pound Jack Crevalle fish from the water. The proud fisherman held his catch high; the Belizean version of a local cat fisherman on the Mississippi Delta.

As we approached the swirling hole, Alberto cut the power and the boat slid in quietly so as not to frighten the inhabitants. We tied up to a partially submerged branch and Alberto whispered, "Beeg tarpon here".

We settled down and stared into the brown water for ten minutes, fifteen minutes.... nothing. Then I saw it, a silver sea monster rolled not fifty feet away. Its gapping mouth was the size of a garden pail!

"We feesh now", proclaimed Alberto.

I pulled out my heaviest fly rod, an 8-wt. bonefish rod that seemed like a soda straw when I thought about the hundred-pound tarpon I'd just seen. Mike and I tied on five-inch baitfish fly patterns and began to cast. We cast for two hours and saw a dozen tarpon roll. None grabbed our flies and it was probably a good thing.

The sun was sinking lower in the tropical sky and it was time to head back to the dock. It would take several hours. As we headed down river, now on a falling tide, I noticed the sky begin to darken out towards the north as heavy clouds moved in. The old inboard motor coughed and hesitated occasionally but kept us moving at a good pace back towards the sea. An hour later the winding river began to open into the bay. Lightning flashed far out on the dark horizon.

27

The motor hesitated again and then sputtered and then stopped running all together. Alberto looked surprised. The tide and growing wind from the northwest pushed us into the wide bay and further away from land as he searched anxiously for the problem. It didn't take a mechanic to figure this one out. "Out of gos mon. No more gos".

Damn, this was not good. We had no radio to call for help, no electronics whatsoever.

Alberto suddenly jumped from the boat into the muddy water that I figured would be deep, far over his head. No, he stood up and the turbulent surface came only to his waist. He tied a rope to the bow and waved for Mike and me to join him. We hopped in and immediately our feet sunk above our ankles in the soft bottom. We struggled over to Alberto and proceeded to help him pull the boat towards a large dead tree that was stuck partially submerged in the bay bottom. The aged wooden boat bucked in the growing wind waves.

The rain began to fall and the remaining daylight dimmed as Alberto considered our predicament. "Dave, you and me get gos. Mike you stay wit son Alberto".

The bay's ragged mangrove and grass shoreline appeared to be about a half mile from our moored boat. We had about an hour before dark. The tide had bottomed out and would soon be rising. There was no time to waste. Alberto and I pushed off on foot across the mushy bottom while the angry water lapped at our waists. My rubber flats shoes offered marginal protection from any creatures that might be down there while my shorts and tee shirt offered none. Adrenaline proved to be a bit stronger than fatigue and we reached the swampy shore just before dark.

"Road dat way" explained Alberto pointing down the marshy shoreline.

We waded further in the marshy grass and I noted strange wide trails not likely made by humans. We shortly approached a muddy creek. Alberto waded out to his chest and then began swimming. "What about the SHARKS and CROCS?" I yelled. But Alberto couldn't hear me in the rising wind; or maybe he did hear me but knew there was no better choice. I did my best to shut down my mind's "imminent danger alert" and jumped in to follow.

Meanwhile Mike was back on the rocking old boat trying to calm a frightened young Alberto in the growing darkness, wind and thunder. Heavy rain began to fall and Mike motioned the boy to take cover with him under the enclosed bow. Verbal communication was minimal, but just after they got out of the rain, young Alberto spoke an unmistakable, "Poop!"

There were a few old newspapers shoved up in the bow and Mike spread one out on the rocking deck. Once Alberto was done with his business, Mike threw the mess overboard. Mike checked the security of the mooring rope one more time. A broken or untied line would send the small boat bouncing and drifting out to sea.

A pelting rain was falling now and all they could do was take cover and wait. Darkness was nearly complete and the only illumination was the small indigo light on Mike's wristwatch. Just as they became somewhat comfortable, Mike felt a crawling sensation on his bare leg. He pressed the light button on his watch just in time to catch a fleeting glimpse of a new horror, a three-inch cockroach scurrying off his foot!

Alberto and I swam two dark creeks and lived to tell about it. We finally made the road at around midnight and Alberto stood by to flag down a passing car. Despite the tropical air, my soaked and tired body began to shiver in the wind and rain. Fortunately, Alberto soon caught the attention of a concerned driver and we headed towards his home.

Alberto lived in a shanty on a narrow canal and there was an aluminum outboard skiff tied to a post. It took Alberto just ten minutes to grab some fresh water, food and two jugs of gasoline. Then we were on our way out to the bay. The ride was rough although the wind showed signs of abating. The natural light was minimal but, being an experienced waterman, Alberto was able to find the wooden boat and its passengers in just a few hours.

Mike and young Alberto we're thrilled to see us. We struggled on the dark bouncing decks to refuel and re-start the boats. Soon we were underway, both Albertos in the aluminum skiff with Mike, me and our brown six-legged passengers following in the sturdy old wooden craft. As the storm began to pass, we entered the calm channel and watched the first glow of morning light towards the east.

I'm heading back to Belize next winter. I think I'll look up Alberto or maybe Alberto Jr. I'm sure he's an expert fishing guide by now.

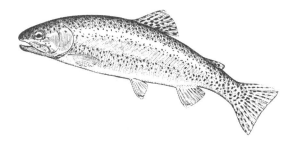

3 MOOSE PIZZA

Alone on the Alaskan Tundra

One of my best college buddies later became an attorney in Anchorage, Alaska. Rob was a fly fisherman and pilot who owned a Piper Super Cub airplane, the VW Bug of the Alaskan bush. Super Cubs are constructed of light steel tubing, plywood and a painted canvas skin that can be repaired in the field with duct tape. With their ultra-slow stall speed they can land on terrain that is too rough for other aircraft.

Rob had the option of either the soft fat "tundra tires" or floats that he could use on his front-and-back two seat Super Cub. I visited Rob many times during summer vacations and we often ventured out in his plane searching for prime wilderness fly fishing. Our range was several hundred miles from Lake Hood, the floatplane base at the

Anchorage Airport. We would need to locate a few of the plastic gas cans Rob had previously stashed at small lakes along our flight path.

Our low-level flights were incredible with sightings of grizzlies, moose, caribou and huge king salmon spawning in tiny feeder creeks barely as wide as the salmon were long. The most spectacular sights were the massive dirty glaciers on the foot of Mt. Denali (McKinley). Gaping fissures, sometimes a thousand-feet deep, were cut by raging rivers of gray glacier melt. I felt tiny floating a few hundred feet above the enormous ice flows. Occasionally during a long flight over easy terrain, Rob would let me fly while he took a catnap. All I had to do was keep the elevation and compass heading steady. It wasn't too difficult or stressful, especially when a tap on the shoulder would get Rob back on the controls.

One late July day we flew to the Talachulitna River a few miles below the lake of the same name. Rob had to return to work at his law firm and left me alone on the riverbank for four days; alone for the first time during my many trips to Alaska. I was excited, but a little nervous as well. Rob helped me unload a small pile of camping and fly fishing gear into the low-lying shrubbery along the shoreline. He climbed back into the pilot's seat and I pushed the Super Cub back out into the gentle flow. Rob cranked up the engine. "I'll see you on Friday!" he hollered above the plane's roar as he taxied out into the river and turned the Super Cub downstream to gain takeoff speed.

Rob pulled the throttle and the little plane, with its lighter load, was soon skipping across the water and then lifting softly off the sparkling surface. The yellow Super Cub gradually faded low towards the horizon until it disappeared.

If you've never been dropped off in a floatplane or helicopter in true wilderness, you haven't experienced that feeling of complete isolation when the sight and ear-splitting clamor of your transportation, your thin link to civilization, is suddenly gone. With just the gentle gurgling of the river remaining, it's a strange mixture of peace, wonder, elation and fear, one of the more intense emotions I've known. Those emotions are greater when your group size is smaller. This time, my group size was one.

After a few minutes mentally adjusting to the solitude and taking in the soft sounds of the wide, shallow river, I got to work setting up my simple camp. There was no good place to erect the small two-person tent due to the rocky ground covered with about six inches of prickly tundra. I settled for a spot right on the riverbank. The tent bottom settled into the vegetation until it was resting at the water level. Fortunately it was a quality tent and no water soaked through the nylon floor.

The weather was the warmest I had ever experienced in Alaska and the mosquitoes were thick and aggressive. Their hum was audible over the babbling flow of the river. I rigged up my 6-wt. fly rod and waded out into the clear current where a slight breeze pushed many of the annoying bugs back towards the bank.

The fishing for fair-sized Arctic grayling, rainbow trout and Dolly Varden was good. My small Adams dry fly rarely went five casts before it was attacked during its gentle downriver drift. But I soon ran into a dilemma. When I waded back a few hundred feet to my tent to take a break, the mosquito swarms tripled. I slipped into the tent but, with the strong sun shining through, it felt like a sauna. A half hour of the heat was all I could take before I waded back out over the fine gravel to the middle of the river for relief. The fish continued to strike as the warm sun energized all the wildlife in the water, air, and on the tundra. Two large jet-black ravens flew by just above me, their caws seeming to mock the lowly fisherman below. I stood in the current for hours catching and releasing fish after fish. It had never happened before, but I was getting a little bored with all the catching. The alternative, however, was miserable.

It reminded me of that story about the old fisherman that had just passed to the great beyond and found himself on the perfect trout stream with a fantastic guide and just the right fly rod. After hours of catching perfect fourteen-inch brown trout on each cast, the fisherman became tired and asked his guide if he could take a short rest break. "No" replied the guide. "You are not allowed to rest here."

The fisherman fished on and continued to catch trout after trout. "I didn't know that fishing could be this good, even in heaven", said the weary fisherman.

"Who said we were in heaven?" responded the guide as his face turned beet red.

I continued to cast until the sun dropped low enough in the sky to cool off the tent.

After a quick dinner, cooked under the rain fly to keep the mosquitoes at bay, I crawled into the tent and zipped the mesh door flap shut. The sun had barely settled below the horizon and the glowing sky was nearly as dark as it would get that night.

For protection from the many creatures that lurked, Rob had given me his trusty Remington 12-gauge shotgun. The shells were loaded with larger BB shot, a recommended Alaskan defense against aggressive grizzlies. I've never been too comfortable with firearms so I left the shotgun unloaded and the ammunition loose on the floor of the tent.

I fell asleep quickly, half in and half out of my sleeping bag. A few hours into a deep sleep I awoke to heavy rhythmic splashing along the river's edge. I listened carefully for a few seconds and knew it was something very large stalking up the river's edge....towards me! I sat up in a flash and was wide awake in a few seconds. I reached for the shotgun and then ran my hand along the tent floor to locate the shells. I grabbed one and prepared to shove it into the chamber. By now I guessed the creature was less than 100-feet away and still moving at a walking pace; splash, Splash, SPLASH. It wasn't an agitated walk but I worried that the loud "CLICK" of the shells entering the chamber would send it into a rage. I loaded the first shell, CLICK, and then a second, CLICK, cringing each time. My heartbeat raced but, fortunately, the pace of the walking stalking creature remained steady. I froze as a massive dark shadow approached the tent and then quietly raised the shotgun. SPLASH, SPLASH, SPLASH. My finger quivered on the trigger.

Then, through the mosquito mesh, two tall gangly legs came into view; long legs leading up to a huge brown torso. I could have reached out and touched the massive moose from the tent. Fortunately for me, it was only on a midnight stroll and not in a fighting mood. Onward it walked past my tent; SPLASH, Splash, splash up the river and into the night.

The next two days went pretty much the same as the first, but without any midnight visitors. The mosquitoes flourished and those beautiful grayling, with their iridescent sailfish-like dorsal fins, continued to grab my #14 Adams off the river's surface. All were carefully released back to the water with the exception of two that I fried-up on the third night. The late evenings were spectacular with the golden glow of the barely-hidden sun pouring over the rolling arctic tundra. Tall ice-capped peaks rose in the distance.

Rob had planned to return by mid-day after my third night out. The weather remained stable and warm. I can't remember another Alaska trip with such a long rainless spell. The day of Rob's return arrived. Noon passed and then 2 PM with no Super Cub in sight. I fished on. Five o'clock came and then 6....no Rob. My food supply by then had dwindled to a small stack of granola bars and a river full of fish. I began to worry. "Where is Rob? Is he OK?" I hadn't notified anyone else about my planned fishing location (It was a mistake and, ever since, I always tell a friend or family member where I plan to be before heading out into the wilderness).

Nine PM came and the sun was low on the horizon. I had spent most of the last three hours scanning the sky in the direction of Anchorage while making an occasional cast in between. Both my anxiety and hunger pangs were growing stronger. Getting out of there and back to civilization on my own was probably impossible.

Then, several miles in the distance, I caught sight of a yellow dot hovering a few hundred feet above the treeless ground. It had to be Rob. A minute later I could make out the shape of the Super Cub. Rob flew directly over me as he inspected the river for obstructions that could interfere with a safe landing on the water. I waded to shore so I wouldn't become an obstruction myself. Rob circled downstream and turned heading upriver towards the long smooth run I'd been fishing. Those rising rainbows were in for a surprise.

The Super Cub glided low and slow; then the two floats kissed the water. The plane skipped for a few seconds and then slowed as the floats grabbed the flow. A moment later it became an airboat and Rob steered on the water with small rudders on the rear of the pontoon floats. He taxied upriver just past me to a gentle backwater. I met him just as the floats nestled into the soft sand and grass along the bank. Rob cut the power and the propeller gradually slowed to a stop. The plane's door popped open and out came Rob's arm cradling a large cardboard pizza box. "Did you order the Pepperoni, or was it Canadian bacon?"

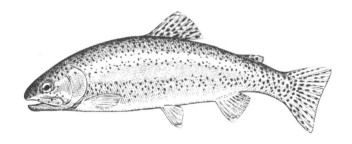

4 BILL'S PATAGONIA

Expedición de Chile

My first business partner Bill was hands-down the most determined and adventurous fly fisherman I've ever known. A most unique individual, Bill was an All American marksman in college, held a Berkeley Doctorate in aquatic ecology and was an ex U.S. Marine. Once a Marine, always a Marine. Every fly fishing trip, no matter how short or long, was planned and executed like a military mission, a great adventure. Bill's gung-ho fly fishing ventures, even those that could be carried out over a weekend, included most or all of the following items: 4x4 vehicles, rifles, ammo canisters, a spotting scope, scuba gear, rubber rafts, walkie talkies, climbing rope, backpacks, machetes, a hydraulic winch, tents, night-vision binoculars and maps with all sorts of added arrows, Xs and notes.

Bill was a generation older than me and, as a young twenty-something fly fisherman, I followed eagerly in his shadow. Bill frequented the Golden Gate Casting Club in San Francisco and was friends with many of the old California fly fishing legends; Mel Krieger, Andre Puyans and Jim Adams. I met them all and even fished with them a few times.

Bill had been an avid big game hunter and deep-sea fisherman but had become primarily a catch-and-release fly angler by the time we met. He had decided that he preferred to release his quarry alive and leave the natural environment in tact after a successful mission. Bill had a strong connection with rivers that continued to grow, and he eventually became a staunch conservationist.

A few years before we met, Bill and his teenage son made an epic six-month-long road trip from near Berkeley, California to road's end near Puerto Montt, Chile. They departed California in late summer and arrived in early-summer Patagonia. Bill had been inspired by Roderick L. Haig-Brown's South American fishing adventures described in the 1954 book *Fisherman's Winter*. He had read it many times over.

With their trusted Toyota pickup, Bill and son encountered Mexican banditos, corrupt Honduran border guards, armed Columbian troops and dozens of friendly villagers everywhere they traveled. They drove through tropical rainforests, over barren high mountain passes and were ferried across the wide Amazon. When Bill and his son reached Chile, they fished Maule Lake, the Laja River, the Lake District and a few Patagonian rivers as far south as the rough dirt roads would allow.

Bill spoke often about his amazing journey to South America, always with a gleam in his eyes. His only disappointment was that he could not reach rivers further to the south that were rumored to hold "puercos del rios", brown and rainbow trout to fifteen pounds and even larger. I was always transfixed by Bill's tales of Patagonia, and jealous too.

During our breaks at work, with my encouragement, Bill and I began to hatch a plan. There were no roads leading to many of those mystery rivers south of Puerto Montt, Chile but perhaps we could access them by sea. A year of research followed. A letter to the Chilean government followed by a five-month wait yielded a treasure; a ten-pound roll of coastal charts and maps, each hand stamped "Armada De Chile". A number of conversations with Mary Crowley of Ocean Voyages in San Francisco led us to "La Guiteca", a 54-foot privately-owned wooden motor yacht berthed in Puerto Montt, Chile.

While planning, we discussed our idea with many fellow fly anglers in the Bay Area, "Join us on the Trip of a Lifetime as we explore the rivers of Patagonia!" We even gave it a name, "Expedición de Chile".

Initial interest into the planned month-long fly fishing adventure was high, but serious interest was less enthusiastic. In the career-oriented world of the San Francisco Bay area, few could imagine taking that length of time off from work and away from their families.

Bill and I sent out letters and made phone calls. We held trip information parties at our homes. After months of recruiting, we found three other experienced fly anglers willing to make the full commitment. Our parties became more serious planning and organizational meetings.

Lists of necessary supplies were written and rewritten. Hours were spent pouring over the maps and charts searching for likely trout-filled rivers. Bill analyzed the maps like a colonel preparing for battle. Rivers with large watersheds and those that flowed out of lakes took priority. Rivers that originated off of obvious glacier fields would likely contain too much glacial flour, ground rock powder, to be good fish habitat. Soon Bill had the maps covered in pencil marks. Some rivers were named and, in our opinion, this probably indicated larger flows; the Palvitad, Yelcho, Palena and, most intriguing, El Rio Tic Toc. Would any of these be a fly angler's river of dreams?

Our knowledge of the fisheries was limited but we knew that many of the largest sea-run brown trout entered the rivers in February and March on their spawning runs. This was fall in Patagonia. Big sea-run brown and, possibly, rainbow (steelhead) trout were the major goal for our journey far to the south.

Trout in Patagonia

Historically, no trout or salmon were ever present south of the equator. This included regions that are prime trout fishing destinations today, New Zealand, Tasmania and Patagonia (southern Chile and Argentina including the island of Tierra del Fuego). In the late 1800s, Patagonian estancia owners originally from Europe conspired to transport the beloved trout of their youth from their home waters to the cool clear rivers flowing from the Andes Range. In the days before modern refrigeration, this was a challenging task. All ships, sail and steam, had to pass through the blistering tropics. How could the living trout or trout eggs be kept cool, oxygenated and alive?

As it turned out, the estancia (ranch) owners produced far more beef than could be sold locally and they had devised "cold hatches" on their ships. These were wooden compartments with ice holds insulated with layers of moss. The cold hatches allowed for the transport of fresh beef from Patagonia all the way north to Europe and the U.S., an ocean voyage of three weeks or more. A few determined estancia owners concluded that the same ships might safely transport fertilized brown trout eggs across the equator from Europe to Argentina and rainbow trout eggs from California to Chile.

Initial success was limited. Many of the trout did not survive the ocean journey and many that did never reproduced. The first rainbow trout hatchery built on the Rio Blanco in 1905 greatly facilitated the large-scale introduction of trout to southern Chilean waters. Soon a few Patagonian watersheds had stable populations of rainbow and brown trout. The trout were more highly evolved predators than the native fish species and thrived. The range of Patagonian trout spread quickly as some were transported by humans while others became anadromous (sea-run) and entered new rivers. Brook trout (char) and Pacific salmon were later transported from North America and thrived in a few Patagonian rivers.

Some of the earliest documented sports fishing in South America was described in Bill's favorite *Fisherman's Winter* written by Roderick L. Haig Brown in 1954. By the 1960s a few adventurous Americans were traveling to Patagonia in search of a new fly fishing nirvana led by the father of American fly fishing Joe Brooks. Brooks made his first trip to Patagonia in 1955 after receiving an invitation from a Buenos Aires native he had met while guiding in Islamorada, Florida. A 1964 episode of *ABCs Wide World of Sports* featuring Joe Brooks and Curt Gowdy fly fishing in Argentinean Patagonia was so popular that it spawned a new television series, *The American Sportsman, that* ran for twenty years. The word was out but the vast extent of potentially great wilderness fly fishing water in the far south had barely been touched.

Preparation

One of our greatest challenges in attempting to explore the rivers of southern Chile was designing and building a transportable jet boat that could be broken down and shipped in reasonably-sized crates, yet have the capability to carry all five of us with gear and fuel up from the ocean into the shallow rivers.

Bill knew what the Marines would use, a Zodiac. So we bought the British version of the French-made Zodiac, a sixteen-foot Avon inflatable with a plywood deck and sturdy transom. The cars were moved out of Bill's garage and we began to experiment. We already owned a 70-HP Johnson outboard and purchased a jet-drive conversion unit to replace the lower propeller-drive. We strengthened the transom with steel struts and lifted the mounting location of the outboard until the jet drive's water intake was only a few inches below the hull. This would allow us to run in water less than six-inches deep.

We constructed a center console steering post with marine plywood. We built and tested wooden seats but decided that it would be better if two anglers sat on each inflated side hull with the fifth standing up at the console and driving. Bill and I towed our experimental jet sled to the American River above Sacramento for a full trial run. We put in at Ancil Hoffman Park where I had spent many hot summer days rafting the rapids as a teenager. We anticipated that the river conditions in Patagonia would be similar.

I had spent so many hours with the design and construction of our inflatable jet sled that Bill assigned me to be the driver. We launched off the trailer and I let the motor idle for a minute as we slowly drifted downstream. Then I buried the throttle. With a roar our experimental jet boat jumped to attention. A few seconds later we were skipping over the water like a thin stone perfectly tossed. It took a few adrenaline-filled minutes to gain control of the skittering craft but then I started to get the hang of it. What a thrill! The cool January air blasted our faces as the gravel bottom flew by just beneath us.

Turning was tricky but I learned to start each maneuver early. The flat hull would slide towards the outside of each bend like a drifting racecar. We stayed in deeper whitewater for a while but I gradually gained confidence and spotted a shallow side channel up ahead. With a quick crank of the wheel we shot up the foot-deep riffle. Our custom jet sled was gliding over water that would barely cover our ankles!

After the initial rush Bill reminded me that caution would have to prevail. This would be our sole method of travel from the mother ship upstream into the remote Patagonian rivers. A broken boat would result in a broken expedition and broken dreams.

A few miles upstream we turned and headed back down through the rapids. Now we were propelled over the gravel bottom with the combined speed of the jet sled and the current. This was no time to strike a submerged boulder or log. The PVC-coated nylon cloth hull beneath the plywood deck was tough but no match for a hard object at 30 mph.

As we approached the launch ramp and our trailer, my heart sank. There stood a Sacramento County Sheriff's officer giving me an angry stare. I'll admit that I had never seen a motorized watercraft on this section of the American River; but given that it was the perfect testing water, I "forgot" to check to see whether it was even legal.

"You can't run a motor boat on this section of the river!" lectured the officer sternly as we pulled up to shore. "I'll have to write you up!"

But Bill, as always, was quick with a response. "We're research scientists from Berkeley preparing for a fish survey in Patagonia; you know, in South America. We're leaving soon and needed to make a test run."

Bill's response wasn't totally dishonest. We did have three biologists on our expedition team and would be collecting data for anyone that might be interested. The officer let us off with a warning and wished us good luck on our journey.

Puerto Montt and Guiteca

The many months of planning, packing and daydreaming blew by and soon we were on our flights from San Francisco to Buenos Aires, Argentina and then Santiago, Chile. Talk among our team was subdued, but the underlying excitement was obvious.

We flew over the Amazon rain forest for hours as patches of deep green forest and winding brown rivers peeked through the cloud cover. I pressed my face against the window as we crossed the Andes in clear sky and I gazed down at the world's second tallest mountain range surpassed only by the mighty Himalayas. Jagged barren granite spires reached to the sky. Small patches of ice at the highest elevations and large white glaciers with gapping blue wounds lower on the slopes fed the many lakes visible to the west.

We landed in Santiago after the long flight and were met at the airport by a friend of Guiteca's owner. Kathy spoke a little English and Bill spoke some Spanish learned during his previous journey to South America. The broken conversation with lots of hand waving and pointing became a common theme of our trip. Kathy and her helper Goya gave us a van tour of Santiago and then shuttled the five of us and our small mountain of gear to the train station. We boarded for the 500-mile overnight ride south to Puerto Montt, Chile.

The journey by rail held surprises at nearly every turn; a rustic village here, a glimpse of the distant Andes there, a massive estancia in the dryer grassy lowlands. The rail cars were apparently 1950s American versions that had long since passed their useful lives in the U.S. and been shipped to Chile. The vintage wood-paneled cars and vast rolling green hills reminded me of the old American West. I imagined a tribe of Sioux hunters stalking a herd of bison. Ancient indigenous people had lived in this part of modern Chile, but their culture is not as well understood as native North Americans and there were no bison.

The train's toilets were unique. Upon lifting the first wooden lid I was startled by the site of blurred rail ties whizzing by. What a simple solution to one of civilization's greatest challenges. There was no odor and no messy waste for the rail company to deal with; and check out all those beautiful wildflowers on the tracks.

Late afternoon approached and we headed to the dining car for a glass of Chilean red wine and an appetizer. Along with a bottle of the rich local Malbec, we were introduced to our first taste of Erizos de Mar, normally just called erizos. We were told that these salted sea urchin eggs and gonads were a Chilean delicacy and highly prized. They had the general texture of raw oysters but were even slimier, fishier and saltier. I quickly slurped one down immediately followed by a large sip of wine, but only for the true Chilean experience.

The sun dipped below the wooded hills as the train rolled south. The last rays of light struck the snow-capped summit of a tall volcanic cone far in the distance. A two-hour steak dinner, more wine, two days of air travel and the gentle rocking of the train soon had me sound asleep in our bunk car. Tomorrow would be a big day.

We arose at first light to the sight of the Chilean Lake District, not unlike our home range the Sierra Nevada. Large sapphire-blue lakes were ringed by saw-tooth peaks. Green meadows filling the landscape were dotted with wildflowers and crossed by clear mountain streams.

It wasn't long before we approached the seaside fishing and shipping hub of Puerto Montt. The sleep and building anticipation had me almost giddy, but excitement was tempered by my concern for the complicated logistics. In my small backpack were long detailed lists of every item we had shipped, down to each bolt, roll of tape, screw-driver and life jacket. Bill and I poured over them one more time.

Each angler was responsible for his own fishing gear. We carried two or three fly rods apiece, mostly 7 and 8-wts. All of us were fly tiers and hundreds of flies made the trip. Most were streamers meant to imitate small baitfish and the pancora crab, the Chilean version of a crayfish.

The train soon slowed and pulled up to the timeworn Puerto Montt station. Several dozen greeters stood on the stained wooden platform awaiting passengers. We stepped out into the cool air that carried just a hint of diesel fuel. Amongst the crowd was a man holding a cardboard sign with the word "Guiteca" handwritten in black ink. The connection had been made! Our mother ship's crew, Juan Rios and Sebastian Soto, were on the platform to welcome us. Two pickup loads later we were on the docks. In a harbor full of assorted old fishing boats and well-used cargo vessels, Guiteca fit in well.

La Guiteca's Capitan Nicolai Novy came up from below deck to offer us each a warm welcome. Juan and Sebastian were native Chileans while Capitan Novy was originally from Czechoslovakia. The captain's Spanish was excellent but he spoke minimal English. Communication amongst us was rudimentary but the combination of Bill's Spanish and the Guiteca crew's enthusiasm made it work. Our two wooden crates and multiple bags of additional gear were loaded on deck as the sun set below mixed clouds in the gray Pacific sky.

Captain Novy showed us around La Guiteca, a slightly upgraded version of a 54-foot wooden fishing boat. This would be our floating home for the next four weeks and it suited our purpose well. The bunks were comfortable and the galley table, lined with aged mahogany paneling, fit all five of us; Bill, Dave W. Jim, John and me with room to spare. I especially liked the below-deck shower located up against the transom. It had a small porthole at eye level with a wooden cover that could be slid open to view the wild Patagonian coast and the glacier-capped Andes Range on the eastern horizon.

After a good night's sleep while still at the docks, we awoke at first light to a flurry of activity. Bill and I assembled our inflatable jet sled that the crew soon named "Delfin" due to its tendency to porpoise up and down on glassy smooth water. The others organized and stowed our gear. Juan and Sebastian loaded six 55-gallon drums of gasoline on board and Captain Novy reviewed his charts.

Delfin would be towed astern of Guiteca and Bill attached the rope harness we had built at home to spread out the wear and friction points. La Guiteca's tender was a sturdy wooden lifeboat with a small Honda outboard held out over Guiteca's stern on davits. When the tender was free, the davits could be used to raise and lower Delfin out of the water. We had hoped to store Delfin on deck as much as possible but the fuel drums took up too much space. Soon Sebastian and Juan were releasing the dock lines and we were finally off.

Our course took us nearly due south and we spent our time rigging gear and taking photos of La Guiteca and Isla Grande de Chiloe to the west. The huge island protected us from the open ocean swells for the first half of our voyage and smaller islands protected us further to the south. Bill and the captain reviewed and finalized the plan for our first three days.

We initially ran two smaller rivers up to about five miles above the coast while Guiteca rested at anchor as close to the rivers' mouths as Captain Novy considered safe. Both of these rivers were on estancia land and we saw a few cattle, but no roads and no humans. The fishing was marginal for a few smaller brown trout but the experience allowed us to fine-tune our operation and prepare for our first major challenge the following day.

Yelcho

Lago Yelcho and Rio Yelcho just below the lake's outlet were reported to be excellent trout fisheries, but the lower twenty miles of Rio Yelcho had not been fully explored or fished. The word was that the Yelcho could not be accessed from the ocean due to the many shallow braids and an island blocking the mouth. That was just the challenge that Bill needed.

We prepared for an early morning launch to reach the shallow braided river mouth at high tide. We loaded extra fuel, a few cans of chili and corn, granola bars, bread, cheese, and two river bags that contained two small tents and a few wool army blankets. We did not plan on staying on the riverbank overnight but knew it was a possibility due to either an equipment breakdown or fishing that was too good to abandon. We also carried a small marine radio that we could use to contact Guiteca until we rounded the first few river bends and lost our signal.

Captain Novy had been able to anchor Guiteca within two hundred yards of the broad shallow mouth of the Rio Yelcho during the previous afternoon. We awoke in the dark and prepared to launch at first light. An hour before high tide we headed out on Delfin.

We choose the channel with the largest observed flow and entered a confusing spider web of waterways. The channel was littered with huge logs and twisted root wads torn from forests upstream. We worked our way tentatively through the braids and were forced to backtrack at least three times.

Bill and Dave W. made a keen observation; the downed logs seemed to frame the main channels. The primary river channels were not always the widest but they *were* the deepest allowing us passage. The riverbanks were mainly dark gravel bars with some marsh grasses but we could see tall green forest several miles in the distance.

Two hours later but only a few miles from Guiteca, we finally entered a wide valley where the many sinuous channels converged; the main flow of the Yelcho. Soon the fly rods came out and I shuttled our group into the best looking runs. The Yelcho is a large freestone river and our group of experienced steelhead fly fishermen met the challenge as they would have on the Klamath, Eel or Russian. Streamers swung on sink tip lines soon had reels and fishermen singing.

Jim hooked the first fish; not surprising as this was Jim Adams; legendary Lost Coast steelhead angler, PhD biologist and worldwide adventurer. The big silver flash shot 50-feet downstream and then vaulted three feet above the flow. We all yelled out "Rainbow!"

Within the next few hours, we gradually made our way upstream and all hooked large rainbow trout over two-feet long. We were only a short distance above the salt and wondered if these might be steelhead making their fall run to overwinter in the deep holes prior to spawning the following spring.

The day passed far too quickly and we were forced to decide where we would spend the night. Captain Novy had told us about a remote lakeside inn on Lago Yelcho. It was accessible only via a gravel road leading from the Argentine border a few miles east of the lake; that is unless you were riding Delfin up from the sea. We burned over half of our available fuel but made the lake and the small inn by late afternoon, over twenty miles from the resting Guiteca.

The innkeeper was surprised to see us but welcomed the "Americanos" with open arms; our common experience throughout southern Chile. The quaint but comfortable accommodations and large meal of Argentinian beef were welcome by us all, especially when we considered our other option of canned beans and tiny tents. The following morning we paid our bill and headed off downriver for more fishing and a late afternoon rendezvous with Guiteca.

We each picked up a few more hefty rainbows on our way down the Yelcho; all carefully released. Jim hooked one so big that it snapped his 7-wt. rod just above the cork. Fortunately, Jim always carried a few spare rods for himself and the team. Brown trout were scarce in the Yelcho. We had expected more encounters with large "trutta marron" but landed just a few smaller specimens.

Given the quality of the fishing and our confidence in re-navigating the lower river maze, we lingered longer than was prudent. We approached the web of tidal channels as the sun hovered low in the west. Bill kept watch for the downed trees and root masses that marked the larger channels and he directed my course. But we soon ran into a new problem; the ebb tide was draining the riverbed. Within an hour even the main channel was too thin to navigate. We had no choice but to head to shore and wait for better conditions.

The scant camping gear came out and we set up a lowly bivouac. Bill grabbed the radio and hiked towards a slight rise where he hoped to contact Captain Novy. There was nothing to do now but bide our time, not an uncommon experience while exploring the unpredictable wilderness. We rested and told stories. A few nodded off. As darkness fell, a layer of cold fog rolled in off the Pacific. Bill returned and had good news. He had contacted Guiteca and they were standing by anxious for our return. Señior Rios promised a large meal whenever we might arrive.

We carried a powerful light on Delfin, basically a 12-volt auto headlamp shoved into a rubber toilet plunger. Wires were taped to the plunger's sawed-off wooden handle and large alligator clips attached to the Delfin's starter battery. I tested the light for the first time in Chile; success!

We all became more active now as the water began to rise. John threw dry leaves onto the surface of the Yelcho and we watched their progress in the beam of our light. Over the next hour, the leaves' rate of downstream drift decreased indicating the acceleration of the flood tide. The water level rose a few inches on a small branch that John had stuck into the sand.

Our fuel supply was very low and we consolidated our last few gallons shaking every drop from the "empty" tanks into my red coffee cup to pour into the primary tank. The tents came down and we headed back out onto the water and into the dark fog. I idled slowly downstream while Bill swung the light from shore to shore. We came to a fork and decided to try the right-hand channel. Ten minutes later we bottomed out into the sand.

I reversed course and we entered the opposite channel. This led to deeper water on the rising tide. Soon we could see the opening of the bay in the lamp's beam, but our visibility was less than one hundred feet. Bill re-contacted Captain Nova and requested "mucho luz" to be illuminated on La Guiteca. We were on our last few tablespoons of fuel.

We motored slowly through the fog straining our eyes for another ten minutes that felt like an hour. It was midnight. Then we caught the hazy glow of a light beam through the fog, Guiteca's searchlight! Soon we could make out the silhouette of our floating base rocking gently at anchor. Never were we happier to see La Guiteca!

Captain Novy met us on the rail with firm handshakes while Señior Soto was a bit more emotional giving us each a hug as we climbed aboard. Señior Rios was in the galley finishing up a grand meal of fresh conger (eel), machos (mussels), potatoes and green beans. We toasted large glasses of Chilean Cabernet to our success. We poured a second round and toasted again.

We awoke later than usual the next morning to the sounds of our crew busy on deck. While Juan Rios was officially the cook and Sebastian Soto the engine man, they often shared duties. This morning they were pulling crab pots and organizing the deck for our imminent departure to a new river, El Rio Palvitad.

El Rio Palvitad

We were shortly underway. Señior Rios prepared a breakfast of eggs and erizos. The sea urchins had been collected by Juan and Sebastian while we were on the Yelcho. Given Juan's obvious pride in his breakfast preparation, we all nodded our thanks and appreciation. Our "enthusiasm" for the erizos proved to be a mistake. The slimy dish began to turn up more and more in subsequent meals. I ate my share and became a little more accustomed to the fishy flavor and slippery texture. My stomach and digestion, however, never fully adjusted.

We arrived at the mouth of the Rio Palvitad the following afternoon. A quick scouting run on Delfin proved the Palvitad's character was nearly opposite that of the Yelcho. The steeper canyon of the Palvitad presented a deep channel directly to the sea. The river water was clear and cold before it mixed with the ocean. A run of only two-miles upstream was halted by a fifteen-foot waterfall that would likely block passage to any trout migrating upriver. The lower river, however, looked promising for the next day's fishing. A light rain began to fall so we headed back to the anchored Guiteca.

As we approached our mother ship we saw Juan and Sebastian further out in the bay trolling from the tender. They arrived back at Guiteca shortly afterward and we walked over to check out their catch. They had trolled large rusty gold spinners on heavy casting rods. Juan held up two fish. Rainbow trout! Big rainbows of five or six pounds each! This was not at all typical. Rainbow trout from a saltwater bay? They must have been steelhead that spent their adult lives close to their natal river; at least that was our best guess.

Señior Rios baked them for our dinner that night. "Trutta deliciosa!" he proclaimed as he presented the serving tray.

Yes, just like salmon. The proper wine was served of course, Chilean Sauvignon Blanc.

We fell asleep that night dreaming of the big rainbow trout out in the bay. What would the Rio Palvitad hold?

We awoke to a cold morning as we were now into the Patagonian fall. As we motored towards the mouth of the Palvitad in Delfin, the panorama was familiar to all who had fished southeastern Alaska. Tall jagged peaks rose in the distance with a few massive white glaciers winding down. Green forests and granite outcroppings dominated the foreground. There were several differences with Alaska however. The Chilean forests had a higher percentage of deciduous trees and their leaves were beginning to turn red and gold. The Patagonian forests had fewer large mammals than Alaska, and no bears. In Chile I never had that sensation that something might be stalking me from the brush as I sometimes do in grizzly country. There *are* predatory pumas in Chile. They are the same species as North American cougars and mountain lions, but are secretive and rarely seen.

We entered the channel of the Rio Pavitad and sped up to the waterfall. The dark sapphire water appeared to be eight-to-ten feet deep and was sprinkled with large boulders. I dropped off two anglers on each side of the river and then beached Delfin slightly down river. We rarely saw rising fish during our Patagonian exploration and the Palvitad was no different.

I strung up my sink-tip line and tied on my most successful fly from the Yelcho; a three-inch long streamer with a peacock-herl wing, silver tinsel body and red tail similar to a classic Alexandra. The fly was cast quartering downstream and then allowed to swing just above the submerged boulders in a hypnotic rhythm; cast, step, swing, retrieve, cast, step, swing, retrieve. My ten-minute trance was abruptly interrupted by a strong tug. The powerful rainbow immediately went airborne and then dove in a swirl of fine bubbles down to the boulders. The tight line went slack.

Just as I began stripping in my fishless fly, I heard Bill call out from across the river, "Big Fish On!"

It was another rainbow trout, and even larger than the one I had just lost. The fish made a low arching leap and then raced downstream until it was nearly parallel with me. Bill ran down the bank chasing his rainbow but was soon blocked by a few willow trees with low branches that reached far out over the river and touched the water. Bill jumped out onto the branches, one hand holding tight to a bouncing limb and the other holding his pumping fly rod. He reached out with his rod arm but it wasn't enough. Bill worked his way a few feet further out over the river on the bucking branches, attempting to clear his fly line around the limbs. He looked right and then left quickly as the powerful fish continued its downstream run taking more line off his reel. With no other option, at least in Bill's ultra-determined mind, he suddenly yelled out "F... it!" and jumped feet first into the icy river after his prize.

I ran towards Delfin to attempt a water rescue. But within seconds, Bill popped to the surface and his boots caught firm gravel. Soaking wet and shivering, Bill waded to shore still battling the tiring fish. Five minutes later the beautiful trout was his. He held it high for me to see and I pumped my fist from across the river.

Then, in the strange way of fly anglers, Bill gently removed the hook, cradled his prize in the water like a newborn baby at baptism, and sent his catch back home alive. I jumped on Delfin to bring some dry clothes and an army blanket across the river to Bill. He had removed his soaked waders and was sitting on a log shivering. "Was it worth it?" I asked.

"Absolutely!"

Each of us landed one or two large rainbows that day and we all felt content as we motored back the short distance to Guiteca.

The night's meal was more fresh trutta along with delicious "hiebas", crab that the crew had caught in their traps while we were out fishing.

We soon had our nightly visit from the captain. Tall and proper, Captain Novy used our voyage as an opportunity to improve on his limited English. During the day while we were on the rivers, he would rehearse a short presentation.

When the five of us gathered for dinner, he would enter with a greeting.

"Hello feesherman. Do you catch big feesh today? Tonight we find Halley Komet in sky. Es my Engleesh goot today?"

We all nodded "Yes" enthusiastically as we sipped our wine. The captain's efforts were impressive and indicative of his determination to make our expedition as successful as he could. We did find Halley's Comet that night, amongst seemingly millions of stars and unfamiliar constellations in the clear dark sky of the Southern Hemisphere.

Tic Toc

Guiteca motored further south the following day headed for, possibly, our most intriguing destination, El Rio Tic Toc. We stopped for a few hours at a small unnamed stream that, again, proved easy to enter. This stream was only about 30-feet wide and we motored just a hundred feet or so above the mouth. I ran upstream as soon as I had beached and secured Delfin. My first cast into a deep run was intercepted by a violent strike. Before I could gain control, the unseen fish shot back towards Delfin and the others. I gave chase all the way down to the salt water where the fish hesitated. Ten minutes later I led the trout into shallow water, a powerful silver sea-run brown trout of about six pounds.

The following day Captain Novy anchored at the mouth of the Tic Toc and we prepared our gear for another longer exploration. We hoped to reach Lago Trebol at the head of the Tic Toc, a distance of about eleven miles from the resting Guiteca according to our charts. A feeder river, El Rio Loro, appeared to originate directly from a large glacier on the Corcovado range and we expected that water to be colored in glacial silt. Above the confluence, we anticipated a clear flow fed by large Lago Trebol which would likely filter out any glacial flour.

The run up river was relatively uneventful but the gray glacial runoff in the lower reaches disguised some barely-submerged rocks and snags that could damage Delfin's nylon hull skin. I drove as cautiously as possible but we were all anxious to get into the upper river. We reached the confluence of the Rio Loro in under two hours and found clear flow in the upper few miles of the Rio Tic Toc. The perfect mountain river averaged about 60-feet wide and was edged in deep green and red-gold forest down to the banks. Small flocks of widgeon and teal ducks occasionally shot up and down the channel.

The upper Tic Toc proved to be the best trout river of our expedition. It consistently produced fish of 20-to-26 inches for each of the five team members, both rainbows and brown trout. We also caught some six-inch smelt-like fish, perfect prey for a large predatory trout.

The fishing was so good that we decided to set up our minimal bivouac camp for the night. The challenge was finding a flat sandy site to set up our tents. Sleeping bags and pads had been ruled out of our scant supplies as being "excessive" so we needed to find some softer ground; a difficult task in this scoured granite glacial valley.

After giving up on the riverbank, we entered Lago Trebol at the head of Rio Tic Toc. I drove Delfin around the rocky shoreline searching for a suitable campsite. The vast deserted lake was surrounded by sharp granite peaks. The jagged Corcovado Mountains to the north were the tallest and covered by thick broken layers of glacial ice and snow; the source of the glacial flour in Rio Loro that colored the lower Tic Toc light gray. We eventually found a sandy bar at the base of a shoreline cliff. This would be our refuge for the night.

Just before dark I hopped back in Delfin and drove to near the Trebol's outlet where I had noticed an especially interesting submerged shelf and drop-off as we entered the lake. I coasted in quietly and shut Delfin's engine down. The silence and sense of solitude in the immense granite and ice cathedral were powerful. It wasn't the first time that such a feeling had poured over me but it had only been in the wildest and most remote places. I can't fully describe it other than to say it was probably some mixture of awe, wonder, freedom, loneliness and possibly a little fear given my thin layer of protection from the full exposure of nature. There was a strong sense of spirituality to the experience.

Delfin drifted slowly on the glassy water and I cast my streamer towards the drop off. Never during our entire expedition did I anticipate the pull of a massive trout as I did here. Everything was in order, the conditions were perfect. I laid out my first cast. Down, down, down sank the fly in the clear dark water. I stripped it back to imitate a baitfish. Again I cast, waited and stripped with that anxious sensation that all fly anglers know. Cast wait strip. Cast wait strip. Nothing! Surprised and disappointed, I motored back to camp trying to convince myself that the experience would make that next hard strike even more rewarding.

After an uncomfortable night on our hard cold sand beds we headed back down to the river. I dropped Bill off in a slow-moving channel that marked the head of Rio Toc Toc. Bill had brought a float tube along and planned to kick downstream with the slow current for about a mile to meet up with the rest of the team at the larger runs where we had caught so many trout the day before.

We continued to hook beautiful wild browns and rainbows in the remote river with absolutely no sign of another human being. Had this river ever been fished before? This is what we had hoped for when we started planning our expedition over a year earlier.

Bill drifted back down to us a few hours later on his float tube with a huge grin. "It was unreal! I couldn't go ten minutes without hooking a big fish!"

As we motored down the river the fishing became progressively slower. The confluence with the glaciated Rio Loro marked the end of our fishing bonanza on El Rio Tic Toc, the river of dreams.

We flew on downriver in the cloudy flow towards Guiteca. As I mentioned before, the speed of skipping downstream at the combined velocity of the river and the jet sled could be hazardous, especially when the water's reduced visibility obscured submerged obstacles. I turned Delfin upstream and backed down on a few of the trickier rapids around boulders and fallen trees. Then, a few miles above Guiteca while roaring down river, we were met by a hard and sudden thud! Fortunately none of us fell in the river though we all wore life jackets for just such an occasion.

I couldn't see the hull damage to Delfin but knew it was substantial by the volume of water pouring in. The inflated hulls remained rigid so there was no risk of sinking. Our only choice was to motor slowly out to Guiteca for repairs. Most of the water drained out through Delfin's check valves as I powered gradually down river. Two hours later we reached Guiteca and tied the wounded Delfin up for the night.

Captain Novy's short dinner conversation focused on his desire to move Guiteca south to Puerto Cisnes to refuel and pick up supplies. The captain recommended that we travel inland to Lago and Rio Rosselot where the owner of La Guiteca, Señior Ibáñez, had caught "truttas grande" the previous year. Señior Soto had a friend with a truck that would transport our team and Delfin to the lake.

The following morning Sebastian lowered the tender into the water while I prepared the injured Delfin to be lifted out using Guiteca's stern davits. Once Delfin was about five feet above the water, Sebastian and I hopped onto the floating tender to make our inspection.

A large fourteen-inch tear was immediately obvious in Delfin's nylon bottom skin where the heavy wood transom met the hull. Another smaller tear of about four inches was found a few feet further forward. We had planned for such an occurrence. Bill pulled out the repair kit and cut large pieces of heavy PVC-coated nylon cloth while I cleaned and trimmed the damaged areas. We followed the directions on the Zodiac repair glue container and had Delfin patched up in just over an hour.

Lago Rosselot

La Guiteca made five stops on smaller rivers during our voyage south to Puerto Cisnes including two on Isla Magdalena. The number of potential trout-filled rivers on the charts of this region were hard to comprehend. Hundreds of complex glacier-carved channels and islands defined the geography. Fortunately La Guiteca's owner and crew had anchored off many of these rivers and fished near the mouths. Captain Novy shared his experiences as we marked up our maps and planned our next few days of exploration.

At each river stop our anticipation was sky high. We never saw another fishermen on these remote rivers. In fact, other than our group and a few anglers fishing conventional gear in the ocean (including Juan and Sebastian trolling for rainbows off the mouth of the Palvitad) we never saw another angler during our journey. Most of the smaller rivers and streams yielded some brown and rainbow trout including a few large specimens that were silver-hued indicating time spent in the sea.

Once we had tied up to the docks at Puerto Cisnes, we were met by a driver with a large flatbed pickup truck. Luis would transport the five members of our team and Delfin to Lago Rosselot. Traveling along the rough dirt road, we came across a farmer and his son riding on an aged wooden oxcart. A single muscular brown-and-white ox with long pointed horns pulled the timber cart with rubber truck tires on rusted steel rims. Luis stopped to speak with the farmer. As it turned out, Captain Novy had arranged that we stay with the farmer and his wife in their farmhouse on the shore of Lago Rooselot.

Alberto and Sonia were fine hosts with very basic accommodations. Their gray bare-wood two-story farmhouse had no electricity or running water. Fresh water was hand-pumped from a small creek and food was cooked on a wood-burning stove. Oil lamps and candles lit up the small dining room at night. Semi-wild chickens and roosters roamed near the farmhouse, kept close by an occasional meal of grain. Various fruit trees and vegetables grew in semi-organized rows on a few adjacent acres. Large Lago Rooselot occupied the foreground out to near the horizon line of grassy hills.

Bill and I slept in two tiny beds upstairs. The thin feather mattresses were hard and lumpy. The upstairs walls were rough unpainted planks. What I remember most though, was the skinned lamb carcass tied to a rafter directly above my bed. The skinless head and eyes were still attached, like something out of a cult horror film. In this case, however, it was all about practicality; a way to keep flies and other pests off the family's forthcoming meals. I pushed the bed a few feet to the side. Sure enough, when we returned from fishing the next day, two legs had been carved off my eerie bedroom pet and they were served to us for dinner. Fortunately a plate of baked trout, fresh from the lake, was also offered.

Fishing in Lago Rooselot was excellent especially in the wide shallow boca, the outlet at the head of Rio Rooselot. The numbers of trout landed were not high but the size was exceptional. Here, John landed the largest trout of our journey, a 32-inch "puerco marron" that must have approached fourteen pounds! I watched the battle with the big trout through the haze of a light rain from across the boca. John's trophy had the yellow-bronze coloration of a resident lake brown trout, not the silver sheen of a sea-run fish.

We also caught native Chilean fish in the Rooselot that Alberto called "perchatrutta", perch trout. Their appearance was something like a walleye. They were clearly no evolutionary or predatory match for the introduced trout from the Northern Hemisphere.

The following morning after a fine breakfast of eggs and potatoes, we paid our small tab and a large tip to our hosts. Luis met us with his truck and we headed back to Guiteca.

Puerto Aysen

Now we were only a day's sail south to Puerto Aysen, the gateway to a burgeoning trout fishery near Coyhaique and the valley of the Rio Simpson. We decided to spend a few days in the Aysen Region before heading back north. This time we left Delfin behind with Guiteca.

Captain Novy arranged for us to rent a car in Puerto Aysen, an old but functional Plymouth Riviera. For three days we explored the Rio Simpson and a few lakes higher up in the valley, a combination of rolling estancia land and forest. The fly fishing did not approach what we had been experiencing on the wilderness rivers but there were some caddis emerging from one of the lakes and we were able to catch a few smaller brown trout on dry flies.

While making the long dark drive back to our hotel in Coyhaique late one night, we had the strangest experience of our journey. The tall forest blocked out nearly all of the scant light from the moon and stars on that cold clear night. We hadn't seen a single artificial light for many miles, for an hour at least. Suddenly, in the distance we could see a broad glow amongst the trees. It reminded me of a made-for-television UFO encounter film.

Dave W. was driving and he slowed as we approached the strange light. It appeared to be only a hundred feet or so into the woods but we could not make out its source. Dave pulled over onto a wide spot on the narrow road. We all jumped out to investigate. We must have felt security in numbers; I'm not sure I would have approached by myself.

As we walked through the trees and towards the light, a tall cliff came into view. It towered high above us. As we moved closer we saw a large cave opening at least twenty-feet high. Inside the mouth of the cave were candles; lit candles; hundreds of them in all sizes. Some were on wooden tables and others amongst the rocks. As we moved closer we could see other objects; a soccer ball, a stuffed toy monkey and a crucifix...more than one crucifix. In the midst of all this was a framed portrait, a portrait of a young boy possibly ten years old. I shivered.

This was obviously a memorial for the young boy who must have died tragically and not long ago. We all spoke softly with respect and did not take photos. The scene felt especially creepy though since there was no sign of any other human activity anywhere near this site. We left quietly without a complete understanding of what we had witnessed.

We departed Puerto Aysen on Guiteca the next day with just one week left in our adventure. We planned on spending another day on the Tic Toc but the weather did not cooperate. It was early April and fall storms began to roll off Antarctica and the Southern Ocean. The last few rivers we explored were high with brown runoff but they still yielded a few trout.

As we motored into Puerto Montt, the onset of winter did not feel far away. The angling season was complete for this year. We celebrated with Captain Novy, Sebastian and Juan on our last night in port and mentally prepared for our return to civilization two days later.

Postscript: Many years after Expedicion de Chile, I received a sad phone call. Bill had drowned while steelhead fishing on Washington's Olympic Peninsula. It was tragic no doubt, but somehow fitting. He died in the natural environment he loved most and he fished to his last hour.

If you've searched the Internet for "Halley's Comet" you already know that our Expedicion de Chile occurred in 1986. That's why we couldn't use a GPS to locate Guiteca in the dark fog at the mouth of Rio Yelcho and why we communicated with written letters instead of texts and email. Dedicated fly fishing lodges in southern Chile were a new concept back then but there are dozens today, including a few on Lago Yelcho. The road system has been greatly expanded and many of the wild rivers we fished are now accessible by car. We never learned how the Rio Tic Toc got its name. It is still remote today, located in Parque Nacional Corcovado.

5 ANOTHER WORLD

Anaa Atoll, French Polynesia

Emerald green clouds beckoned ancient South Pacific mariners from far out at sea; the reflected light off the shallow tropical lagoon of Anaa Atoll. The remote Polynesian Island was infamous for its fierce and brutal warriors when first discovered by European explorers in the 1600s. Rumors of cannibalism at that time and place in Polynesian history are still whispered today.

My long-time fly fishing friend Mike and I had the opportunity to be among the first to fish the warm sand and coral flats of Anaa as a test to determine the viability of a possible new fishing lodge. Our primary targets were bonefish and trevally but we were just as interested in experiencing a remote South Seas island culture.

After a long flight from Los Angeles to Papeete, Tahiti we boarded a local island hopper for the 200-mile flight east to remote Tuuhora, the only village on Anaa with a population of less than 500. As always, we sat in window seats and pressed our faces against the glass. The small plane flew over the deep blue tropical Pacific at a level just below the clouds. Dots of coral islands occasionally came into view. Most appeared uninhabited but a few had villages visible from the air. Some were groups of many narrow islands arranged in large rings or ovals; coral atolls.

A coral atoll is formed when the central core of an ancient volcanic island subsides slowly into the sea over thousands of years. The outer living ring of island coral continues to grow upward and outward as quickly as the dead volcano sinks resulting in a coral band encircling a shallow central lagoon. Passages from the lagoon to the open ocean allow seawater and fish to enter and exit the protected saltwater lake on the tides. The result is a perfect tropical environment for bonefish, trevally and fly anglers.

We were over the Tuamotu Archipelago now and portions of a large atoll came into view; Anaa. The plane descended low over the eighteen-mile-long lagoon. The water, depending on the depth, was varying shades of off-white to emerald green to turquoise. Brown living coral grew in uneven mounds within the deeper zones.

White sand beaches appeared on the fringes of narrow strips of land. Tall sweeping coconut palms reached high into the humid trade winds. Soon we were at eye level with the palms and then the tires met the hard runway. The landing strip was bordered on one side by the dark blue South Pacific Ocean and by Anaa Lagoon on the other.

Hot sun and a warm tropical breeze greeted us along with a Tahitian welcoming committee of local villagers. Pungent red flower leis were draped around our necks as we stepped off the ramp. Oliver, the fly fishing business manager and one of just a few non-Polynesians on the island, introduced himself with a smile and brisk handshake.

Our gear was loaded into a rusty white van for the short ride into the village. Bright red hibiscus and white frangipani flowers lined the narrow coral soil roadway while a few local children ran alongside and waved. We grinned and waved back. Some small colorful homes came into view scattered among the palm trees.

The van parked at a small blue two-story bungalow, our home for the week. Each level held a mattress lying under a flowing tent of mosquito mesh. Two fat-tired bicycles leaned against the porch; our transportation around the village. So far it was everything that we had hoped for. Would the fishing be as good?

Oliver helped us unload and notified us that our fishing guide was ready to take us out on the lagoon for the afternoon. We could eat lunch at the dining area or take a sack lunch and head out now. We had Oliver take us straight to the boat.

Our guide was Vaea and he welcomed us with a broad Polynesian smile. Dark, young and heavily built, Vaea was barefoot with faded green shorts, a burgundy T-shirt and blue baseball cap. According to Oliver, Vaea was an expert fisherman but had little guiding experience. Oliver went on to explain the island language.

The people of Anaa spoke a combination of Tahitian and French. It made sense because Anaa is officially one of the many islands that make up the country of French Polynesia. Oliver was French Canadian so he communicated with the islanders in French. Mike and I speak neither French nor Tahitian so we fell back on the hand gestures that we had used with partial success at Christmas Island a few years earlier.

We soon learned our first Tahitian word from Vaea as he waved us towards the boat and pointed out into the lagoon...."Kio Kio", bonefish.

The boat was a sixteen-foot fiberglass outboard skiff with an elevated stern poling platform. With his long wooden push pole, Vaea could quietly move the skiff along on the shallow flats while we searched for bonefish. There was a stern seat, a wooden center seat and an elevated bow casting deck for one angler.

We sped out over the smooth surface of the sparkling ocean lake. The moving air felt good under the hot South Pacific sun. The mixed white sand and coral bottom was nearly always visible through the shallow crystalline water. The entire Anaa lagoon is fringed by swaying coconut palms but they were not visible on the horizon due to the vast distances from one side to the other. It seemed like the areas to fish would be endless.

Twenty minutes later Vaea cut the outboard power and we coasted silently onto a white sand flat. The outer edge of the shallows was chest deep, so we started out casting from the bow of the boat one at a time. Our only previous experience fishing the flats of the tropical Pacific had been at Christmas Island and our fly selection now looked similar; Crazy Charlies, Christmas Island Specials, Moana's Chili Peppers and Gotchas in several weights and sizes.

Mike took the elevated bow platform first and stripped 60 feet of fly line off his reel and laid it onto the deck in loose coils. Polarized sunglasses on, he held the fly in his left hand and gazed through the nearly invisible water.

I stood on the middle seat scanning for cruising fish while Vaea, with the best pair of spotting eyes, pushed us slowly along from the elevated stern platform. A whisper of warm air disturbed the water's surface just enough to warp our view of the sandy bottom in gentle waves. We stared for five, ten, fifteen minutes but no kio kio were spotted. We did see fish; big blue parrotfish crunching on coral and transforming it into white sand after digesting the living polyps. This is the unique source of most tropical white sands.

With a downward push of his open palm, Vaea motioned that we were at low tide. He restarted the motor and moved us across the huge flat onto a shallower area where we could fish on foot. Mike and I zipped on our neoprene and rubber flats booties to protect our feet from sharp coral and any stinging or biting creatures that might be resting on the bottom. As soon as our skin made contact with the water we could tell that it was very warm, almost hot. It was likely too warm even for bonefish. As we expected there were no kio kio so Vaea moved us closer to a deep channel that was now beginning to flood onto the flats. After impaling his push pole into the sand, he tied the skiff off and all three of us hopped out into the knee-deep water.

We waded slowly through the firm sand, Vaea in the middle with Mike and I flanking him about twenty feet to each side. Just as we realized that the fresh tidal flow was cooling the shallows, Vaea called out "kio kio" and pointed at ten o'clock. Four bonefish were approaching me at 50 feet. After two false casts to extend the line, my fly was sent towards the slowly-cruising bonefish and it landed ten feet in front of their noses. The two lead fish darted forward towards the sound of the tiny splash but stopped short. I gave life to the shrimp-like imitation with long slow strips of the line. The two fish, and then a third, rushed and nosed up to my fly as it moved along the bottom. Surprisingly, all three turned away.

Just then Mike released his cast in their new direction of travel. Two strips later one saw his fly and veered right. Halfway through the third strip Mike's line went tight and he was on! The silver kio kio rocket shot across the flats, instantly taking the line into the backing. Mike lifted his hand off the reel momentarily to avoid the spinning handle. He went back to work and gained line, but then the bright flash ran again, although not so far this time. Three long runs later the nice bonefish came to hand and Vaea removed the fly. After a photo of Mike with his first Anaa kio kio, the bonefish was released back to its home. We each had success and landed a few nice three-to-four pound silver torpedoes over the next hour. For each bonefish landed, one or two would be broken off during their initial jet-like acceleration or when the fish zig-zagged through sharp coral and sliced the leader. The immediate sense of disappointment rarely lasted long; the next opportunity was likely to come soon. The tropical sun settled low behind a bank of clouds and Vaea signaled that it was time to head in.

A larger yellow plank home near the skiff's mooring beach was the makeshift headquarters for the proposed fly fishing lodge. Bright flowers and flower prints were everywhere. A tin-roofed partially-enclosed patio was our dining room. It appeared to be a local meeting area and restaurant although there were no menus, signs or prices anywhere.

The owner of the home introduced himself as Manu. "Hello, welcome to Anaa."

Manu spoke a few words of English and carried himself as a humble leader. Dark, fit and middle-aged, his short black hair and straight posture spoke of quiet self confidence. We would spend many fine hours with Manu over the week.

We toasted with Hinano beer and its brightly-colored Tahitian hula girl logo on each bottle. It was one of only a few signs of modern commerce that we saw during our entire stay on Anaa, the complete antithesis of our home state of California.

The following morning we were interrupted from our deep sleep by the loud crowing of roosters at first light. Ten minutes later we were on our bicycles headed to the dining patio and lagoon a half mile away. The quiet village had yet to awaken except for some roaming chickens that scattered as we approached on the white coral-stone road. Early orange sunlight poked through the low billowy clouds and coconut palm silhouettes. The humid breeze was already warm.

Vaea, Oliver and his assistant Linda, another English and French speaker, met us in the dining room for breakfast and a strategy session. Oliver had already learned of the excessive heat on the lagoon flats during the high and ebb tides. It would limit our fishing options until more favorable tides came later in the week.

The island pace was usually slow but Vaea was anxious to get out on the water before the sun rose too high. Always more interested in fishing than eating, Mike and I made quick work of our breakfast of eggs and fried bananas. Linda, in her long blue flowered dress, met us near the skiff with sack lunches and wishes of success.

We fished some closer flats early and picked up a few more kio kio. In the strange way of new friends from different cultures, Vaea was now calling them "bonefish" while we said "kio kio".

The high tide came early and, with the blazing tropical sun, quickly heated the water to a point where the bonefish left the shallow flats to find deeper cooler channels. Under the scattered light green clouds, we explored a small section of the huge lagoon and shot many picturesque South Pacific images; infinite combinations of clear water, clouds, white sand, coral, colorful birds, palm trees and sunshine. Any portion of the daytime sky not covered in emerald clouds was always deep blue, not surprising since this is about as far as you can be from the industrialized world without heading out into space.

Vaea motored over to a deeper area in the lagoon and drifted while Mike and I snorkeled over a few coral heads. Small fish of every color sprinkled the coral like a birthday cupcake. Larger Bluefin Trevally, a great sport fish and Polynesian delicacy, swam in schools nearby. Blacktip Reef Sharks circled out a little further. They showed little interest in our presence but kept us on high alert. Their bodies were a bit smaller than ours but we imagined their teeth to be both larger and much sharper.

We decided to head in early and Vaea sped us back to the village. Several small boats rested at the mooring. Children swam and laughed in the tranquil water while schools of small fish darted around their feet. Even though the protected Anaa Lagoon is massive in area, the ocean tidal passes are shallow and do not allow entry by larger vessels. The only safe landing for supply boats is a concrete wharf and slight indentation in the outer coral reef on the lee side of the island. Even a remote South Seas village requires flour, rice, building materials, and fuel for generators, outboard motors and the few vehicles on the island.

We met Oliver and Manu on the dinning patio. It was clear by now that late morning and afternoon bonefishing would not be productive for a few days until the tide cycle shifted. We needed morning flood tides to push cooler ocean water onto the flats. It was disappointing news but, as is often the case, turned into a blessing as Oliver and Manu had planned other island activities.

Manu was a former champion of "Patia fa", the Polynesian sport of throwing spears at a single coconut husk mounted on a tall wooden pole. I had seen this on a National Geographic TV special as a kid. Would we like to learn? Yes!

Manu had brought some of his hand-built spears, five-foot long hardwood sticks with sharp iron tips lashed to one end. We started our first basic lesson which Mike and I called "Patia fa 101". The spear was held lightly in the left hand, palm up, a few feet below the tip. The left arm was held downward while the left forearm was adjusted up-and-down depending on the height of the coconut target. The spear's thrust came from the middle finger of the right hand also held palm up. The right arm was held low and the middle fingertip rested on a notch cut into trailing end of the spear. Then it was just a matter of stepping forward and throwing the spear with a long underhand sweep of the right arm. Manu made it look easy but it definitely was not.

The target was a green coconut with the soft fibrous husk still attached. For our introduction, the coconut was laid on the ground, a much easier goal than the regulation target mounted on a ten-meter-tall pole. Over the next four days, Mike and I spent nearly as much time tossing spears at coconuts, Tahitian style, as we did casting a fly rod. It was every bit as challenging as trying to place a fly in front of a moving bonefish at 80 feet in a strong crosswind.

We arrived for dinner as the sun set below the horizon; always a magical time of day when the tropical heat was replaced by cooler island breezes, swaying coconut palms, and a call of "ki-ki-ki-ki" from the birds in their fronds, blue and white Tahiti Kingfishers. Mike and I called them "racket birds". Our meal that night was the Tahitian treat of "Ioata", ahi tuna marinated in lime and coconut juice. All of the food on Anaa was fresh, local and delicious; Mahi Mahi, lobster, shrimp, chicken, pork, papaya and coconut.

The following morning we took a longer scenic bicycle route around the village and noticed large areas of old coconut palms arranged in neat rows. Some appeared healthy while others, maybe a third, were dead trunks with no head of palm fronds at all. We eventually learned that these palms told two stories.

Over two hundred years ago, Anaa became a South Pacific farm of sorts. The relatively rich soil, at least by tropical atoll standards, supported the cultivation and preparation of copra, sun-dried coconut. Copra farming peaked in the mid-1800s when Anaa had a population of about 2,000 villagers, more than four times the number now. This accounted for the neat rows of coconut palms. The dead trees told a more ominous tale.

Violent Pacific hurricanes inundated low-lying Anaa in both 1878 and 1906. The winds were strong enough to rip the tops off of palm trees. Huge storm waves washed completely over the atoll and drowned many of the islanders who had no sanctuary from the fury. In a solemn and determined response, the survivors who chose to remain on Anaa constructed a sturdy concrete community center and church on the highest ground in the village; a refuge from the wrath of future hurricanes.

After some morning spear tossing, we changed our fishing strategy and motored out of the lagoon and into the ocean. The outboard propeller barely cleared the white sand bottom of the shallow pass out of the ocean lake. The water was as clear as a swimming pool. This time we carried heavy 12-wt. fly rods and six-inch-long baitfish fly patterns. Our target species were Giant Trevally, the predator thugs of tropical reefs that can grow to 100 pounds and larger. We cruised slowly outside the lee-side drop offs and made occasional casts towards the coral followed by fast strips back to the boat. The visibility of the blue-green water was at least 80 feet. We floated high above ornate coral formations of many colors and shapes; fans, antlers, brains, soft mounds and more. The ever-present emerald green clouds drifted high above the shallow lagoon inside the circling reef.

There was plenty of life out on the reefs; more sharks, barracuda and parrotfish but no trevally that we could find. We did land some heavy snapper-like fish but returned them back to the water after Vaea motioned a warning. They must have been poisonous. It could have been ciguatera toxin that sometimes builds up in the flesh of near-shore predator fish.

Later that evening, since the heavy rods were already rigged up, we decided to make some casts from shore on the ocean-side reef. A short bike ride from our bungalow took us to a likely looking spot where, unlike the protected lagoon, the tide and current churned the water's surface. Top-water plugs seemed like a good choice; the noise might attract a predator fish hunting in the fading light. From the coral rocks, we cast the big rods and chugged the plugs back in until our arms ached, but to no avail. Then, in the last minutes before dark, a huge boil erupted at the end of my line. Fish on!

Rhythmic tail pumps indicated a big fish, but it didn't run with quite the power of a typical Giant Trevally. Fortunately, the fish stayed near the surface instead of diving towards the sharp coral. The heavy leader allowed for maximum pressure and the mystery fish slowly gave in. Standing in knee-deep water, I could finally make out the long slender shape; barracuda! This one was nearly five-feet long. Mike shot a few quick photos and then jumped into the water where we both nervously held the long silver and black body until it revived. The hook was carefully, very carefully, removed from between long dagger teeth and the stunned fish swam slowly out into the darkness.

We rode our bicycles home under the darkest and clearest South Pacific skies I had ever experienced. With nothing to mask their glow, tens of thousands of stars were so bright that we could have been space travelers far from planet earth.

The following day was Sunday and no work was allowed, not even fishing. We feasted with our island friends and then, with their invitation, walked to the sports field. Like the village roads, the flat field was primarily hard white coral soil with worn patchy grass covering a portion. Coral stone walls below bright red and pink flowers formed a perimeter.

The large field was unofficially divided into two sections. On one end was a makeshift soccer goal of old unpainted lumber. On the other, a lashed wooden pole topped by a coconut target stood over 30-feet tall; Patia fa! The pole was raised, lowered and supported with rope guy lines.

Manu introduced us to a few of the local islanders, most barefoot and shirtless wearing only bright shorts. Each had his own supply of custom hand-built spears with individualized markings. The rules allowed each thrower ten shots with the entire group throwing one shot at a time in ten rounds. After the completion of ten rounds, the pole would be lowered and each spear strike tallied.

In a strong competition, more than twenty spears might be stuck in the coconut husk after ten rounds. There were five in our group not including Manu, who coached his new American team of Mike and me. We focused like Olympic contenders; beads of perspiration running down our foreheads under the blazing tropical sun. A small group of villagers stood by as spectators, increasing the pressure on us to perform.

The small green target was located 70-feet horizontally and 30-feet vertically from the competitors. The locals' accuracy was remarkable. They struck the coconut on about one of three throws and came very close or glanced off the coconut on others. Sometimes a previous strike would be nullified when another spear knocked it out of the coconut. My tosses were weak although I did come within about twenty feet of the coconut in the later rounds. A few of my errant spear throws landed frighteningly close to the pickup soccer match...Yikes!

Mike's tosses were more accurate and he actually caught the edge of the coconut with one spear. The spear stuck for a brief moment....but then sagged and dropped off the coconut target to the ground far below. A moan rose from the village spectators, the same in any language. I turned and could see a few nodding in approval. It must have been Mike's baseball experience as a high school shortstop. I awarded him the title of U.S. Coconut Spearing Champion, master of Patia fa.

The following day we focused on Bluefin Trevally in the deeper areas of the lagoon. The beautiful Bluefin are iridescent light blue peppered with black spots. The rule was that you could catch them if you could find them. Competition for food is high among the predatory sharks, barracuda and trevally and the Bluefin Trevally aggressively struck any bright baitfish pattern that was stripped rapidly through the depths. Bluefin Trevally are great sport fish on an 8-wt. fly rod, the largest we encountered being about ten pounds. I have a photo of Mike and Vaea holding a nice Bluefin with the rear third completely gone, replaced by a perfect half-circle bite mark. Vaea kept the trevally as they are prized for their flavor.

Earlier that morning, Linda had promised us a Tahitian surprise at noon. Vaea pulled our skiff up to a perfect white sand South Pacific beach, deserted except for Oliver's small boat. Linda, Oliver and a young village woman, Palila, came out from behind a breadfruit tree to welcome us as we approached. Linda announced that we were to be treated to a traditional island meal just like the ancient Polynesians.

A fire was started on the beach with old coconut shells as fuel. Coral stones were arranged around the fire pit. Palila made plates and cooking trays by interweaving palm fronds together. A few of the whole trevally were placed on the frond mat and then over the fire to bake. Golf ball-sized sea snails were collected off nearby rocks and placed on the hot stones surrounding the fire pit.

Fresh coconuts were opened, the sweet milk used as a marinade for the fish while chunks of the white meat were served as an appetizer. Steamed starchy breadfruit and fresh papaya completed the native feast; all delicious except the chewy sea snails and they weren't too bad. Everything was served on our woven palm frond plates and eaten with our hands. We sat on downed palm logs with our bare feet in the warm tropical water where we could rinse our sticky fingers to the delight of some tiny tropical fish. Could there be a more memorable meal? Mike and I didn't know it at the time but we would have another close encounter with beautiful Tahitian Palila a few days later.

The longer period of flood tide the next day meant that we could once again hunt kio kio on the shallow lagoon flats with a good chance of success. About 30 minutes from the mooring we motored slowly through a rocky area near the palm-covered interior shoreline. Hundreds of coral stones were arranged in unnatural large Vs within the shallows. The narrow V tips opened into small round stone-lined holding ponds. A rough shack on the shoreline was surrounded by weathered wooden frames. They were fish drying racks for bonefish. At least a dozen split kio kio hung to dry. The operation's haggard owner surrounded by a pack of mangy dogs gave us a long stare and insincere wave as we passed. The 30-foot-long stone Vs were bonefish traps no different than those used by ancient Polynesians a thousand years ago.

Bonefish are a favorite meal of indigenous people in many tropical regions where they are found. This is true of the Bahamas, Christmas Island and, as we had just learned, on Anaa. Bonefish harvesting has created a shortage of the prized sport fish in some areas. While the native people have the moral right to the resource, the economic benefit of hosting international catch-and-release fly anglers is usually greater for the local communities, and definitely more sustainable. This is the win-win concept of ecotourism. The people of Anaa Atoll lived primarily a subsistence lifestyle relying mainly on what they could harvest and catch. Some low-impact tourism could improve the minimal island economy. Mike and I were part of that equation.

Vaea moved on and we were soon approaching a picture-perfect white sand flat. The small shallow bay was fringed with coconut palms and looked to be totally deserted except for a quaint and unexpected sight, a tiny old South

Seas stone church. There was no one around and we could not tell how the parishioners might get to this little piece of heaven.

We would be wade fishing but I stood on the bow platform holding my fly rod to observe as Vaea backed off the power and we coasted towards the shallows. It had tied on a #6 tan Crazy Charlie with light bead chain eyes meant for fishing in water of two feet or less. Then, seemingly out of nowhere, I spotted a huge kio kio resting on the bottom in five feet of water; the largest bonefish I had ever seen! The skiff was still moving and my lightweight fly would not get down to the fish. Nevertheless, I reflexively made a quick cast and the fly landed high above the big bonefish. Vaea cut the power.

Bonefish nearly always feed on or near the bottom so I held no hope that I would hook this fish. Amazingly, however, this bone made like a rainbow trout on a mayfly hatch and headed straight up through the water. A foot below the surface, my Crazy Charlie disappeared into the mouth of the huge kio kio. In my shock, I set the hook a fraction of a second late. The bonefish, that I estimated at twelve pounds, spit my fly out and swam off unscathed. It had all happened in less than five seconds; all in full vivid color. Disappointed, I reminded myself that these unexpected moments always keep fly fishing interesting.

Vaea tied up to his push pole in two feet of water and we jumped out onto the hard sand bottom. I spotted the first bonefish off to my right even before Vaea. This time the light Charlie was the proper fly and I sent it on its way. The bonefish turned away as my fly landed so I stripped it in quickly and cast again. It landed a little further in front of the cruising fish and I had a few seconds to wait. When the bonefish was two feet behind and moving towards the fly I made the first short strip. A small puff of sand erupted just like a fleeing shrimp and immediately the kio kio was on my fly. Fish on!

It shot out towards deeper water with my reel screaming in response. About 150 feet out the speedy bonefish slowed. Ten minutes later the back-and-forth battle was over and Vaea carefully released my temporary prize. This was the epitome of bonefishing requiring the focus and stealth of hunting, but with a non-lethal outcome; and all in one of earth's most spectacular natural environments.

The next hookup was Mike's and this bonefish ran even further. It seemed heavy but the flash of silver was so fast that it was difficult to tell. I photographed the action with the perfect South Seas island backdrop. Fortunately there was no living or dead coral on this flat because the powerful fish would surely have run the thin leader over the sharp edges to free itself. Eventually after four long runs, the heavy kio kio was brought to hand, a sure ten pounder!

After landing and releasing a few more fish we made the long run back to the village. This was our last night on Anaa and Linda had asked us to wear our nicest shirts to dinner. We bicycled back to our bungalow and cleaned up in the outdoor shower. Water was supplied from a storage tank plumbed to collect rainwater off the corrugated metal roof, a typical South Pacific fresh water system.

We met back at the dinning patio with all of our new friends; Vaea, Manu, Linda and Oliver among many others. There were more fresh flowers and, combined with the aroma of sweet steamed fish, our senses stirred.

"Welcome to the Tamaaraa, the island feast!" toasted Oliver with glasses of coconut rum.

Oliver and Linda translated as we all sat around the large table recounting our adventures on Anaa. Manu asked that we return to practice Patia fa and to fish with him for Mahi Mahi on the open Pacific, from a speeding boat with spears no less! We thanked Vaea for his efforts as a fine fishing guide. We thanked everyone many times over for their friendship. We ate coconut shrimp, steamed fish and suckling pig wrapped in banana leaves and roasted in an underground oven Hima'a style. The deserts were puddings and cakes made of sweet island fruits.

The celebration lasted well into the evening. Vaea and a friend played South Seas tunes on a guitar and ukulele and we all sang or hummed along. The finale was a half hour of sensual Tahitian hula dances performed just feet away from our wide eyes by beautiful dark-skinned Palila who we learned was Vaea's younger sister. She wore mainly flowers and long black hair.

It was quite a Polynesian sendoff from the beautiful people of a remarkable South Pacific island gem. Uua he-re vau ia oe Anaa!

Postscript: Fly anglers still visit Anaa Atoll on occasion, but due to its remote location, inconsistent fishing conditions, and native practice of harvesting kio kio, no permanent fly fishing operations exist. You can see the emerald clouds of Anaa from the comfort of your home. Search "Anaa Atoll" on Google Earth and note the clouds over the southern lagoon in the 2019 satellite photograph.

6 SELF-GUIDED BY AMATEURS

Big Rainbows, Bigger Salmon and Huge Bears in Alaska

You can experience the wilderness at hundreds of spectacular places around the world. If you want to take the ultimate wild step and be *part* of the wilderness, head into the heart of grizzly country.

The move from Berkeley to Southern California was one I often regretted, and not just because of the culture shock. In Northern California I could always find an adventurous friend to join me on a fly fishing trip to the Tahoe area or Yellowstone National Park; but not down here. It was becoming obvious to me that pursuing money was less important than pursuing passion. No one I'd met down south had my level of enthusiasm for fly fishing, that is until I met Mike. We worked for the same company and were both transplants to Southern California; not a trout fishing paradise but within range. Mike had fly fished throughout Northern California since he was a boy and was a good fly tier as well.

The two of us made quite a few road trips driving five hours or more north on US Highway 395 along the foot of the jagged eastern Sierra Nevada range and its small mountain towns; Independence, Tom's Place, Bishop, Mammoth, Lee Vining, and our favorite, Bridgeport. There are several lifetimes worth of fishing and backpacking adventures available high in those glaciated granite valleys and we explored many. Occasionally when we had a few extra days to hike and climb, we would reach the elusive golden trout.

Not counting a few broken fly rods and flat tires, our trips were always a pleasure and we were constantly planning the next. But the long drives gave us plenty of time to plan even greater fly fishing adventures. The discussion often turned to Alaska. It seemed like simple logic; the more remote and vast the wilderness, the better the fly fishing.

We decided that a lodge wouldn't give us the adventure we were looking for. Mike and I wanted full Alaskan wilderness immersion (while keeping our wader tops above the waterline at all times, of course). We wanted more fish and fewer anglers, a full dose of unspoiled nature. And besides, we could do two or three self-guided Alaska trips for the cost of one lodge trip.

We poured through books and fly fishing magazines for more information on Alaskan wilderness fishing. Actually, we had been doing that for years. This was in the early days of the Internet and only a tiny fraction of the information you can find today was accessible on our original Macintosh computers and early modems.

Our break came from the pages of the *Anglers Report* where fly fishers submit first-hand reports about their fishing adventures throughout the world. One bit of print caught my attention immediately. Alaskan fishing lodge owner and bush pilot Dave Egdorf was offering to fly anglers into the remote Nushagak River headwaters during midweek when his lodge duties were a little lighter. I called Dave during the winter at his home in Montana to get the details. He would supply the raft, ice chest and floatplane flights into the upper Nushagak and then, days later, out of the middle Nushagak about 80-miles down river. The rest was up to us.

Mike and I had accumulated quite a stack of research paperwork by then. We decided to fly up to Alaska at the end of August and spend eight days floating, camping and fly fishing down the river on our own. By late summer, we figured, the mosquito swarms would be decreasing, the rainbow trout fat, the coho salmon running up river, and most importantly, the huge brown bears (AKA grizzlies) would, at least in theory, be stuffed and docile after a summer of gorging on salmon. It seemed like a good plan.

Our preparations gained momentum by late spring. There were long lists of items to consider. Egdorf's Cessna 185 floatplane had weight restrictions so we needed to pack sparingly. On the other hand, if we needed something out on the river that we didn't bring along, we were out of luck. We sorted through our backpacking gear and added some additional camping gear; a larger tent, ultra-light folding chairs and a small roll-up table. We added rope, extra waders, dry bags, mosquito head nets, first aid supplies, USGS topographic maps, and a small folding saw like the one I had in Boy Scouts. We made up a lightweight repair and emergency kit with nylon patches, needle & thread, hose clamps, super glue, duct tape (of course), shoe goo, vinyl electrical tape, fire-starter gel and parachute cord. We prepared a menu that emphasized fresh food early in the trip with more canned and boxed meals later on as the ice in our ice chest melted.

Mike and I tied flies, dozens of them; purple egg-sucking leeches, Mylar-bodied white zonkers, popsicles, pink and cream flesh flies, orange glow bugs, candy canes, black string leeches, deer hair mice, fuchsia bunny leeches, and even a few hot pink floating deer hair polywogs for enticing big cohos to the surface. Fluffy remnants of pink, white and purple marabou feathers, hackle fibers and fur could be found in every corner of my house. On a few early summer days, Mike and I tied in his backyard while discussing our highly anticipated adventure over cold beer.

We packed extra sun glasses and promised each other we would wear glasses at all times while fishing. I had read about a similar float trip that had become a three-day nightmare. While casting on a remote Alaskan river, a fly fisherman had sunk a streamer fly into his own eyeball. The barb held the big hook firmly in place. The pain and agony were intense. It took three frantic days for his partner to row their raft downstream to find help. It's hard to imagine the horror of that experience. Bad things could happen out there.

We had one more important consideration that weighed on us. How should we deal with the huge brown bears we expected to encounter along the river? Since we would be deep in the Alaskan bush completely on our own, we decided to go big. Mike had an old but reliable Winchester 12-gauge shotgun. With a hacksaw, he cut ten inches off the barrel. Mike packed a dozen shells loaded with heavy buckshot. In my experience, the more you're prepared for trouble, the less likely it is to occur.

All of the preparation would have been hard work if we were being paid. For us, though, it was always a pleasure and it kept our level of excitement high for months.

The day finally came and we flew up to the small fishing village of Dillingham, Alaska on Bristol Bay. It was late in the season and nearly all of the commercial salmon fishing fleet had been hauled out for dry storage during the long winter soon to come. Kim Egdorf met us and shuttled our gear 25 miles on a muddy road to Aleknagik Lake for our rendezvous with her husband Dave and his Cessna floatplane.

Tall and full-bearded Dave Egdorf greeted Mike and me on the beach with strong handshakes. In boot-foot hip waders, he wasted no time loading the plane; a hard-working man on a mission. Egdorf was soft-spoken and confident with a streak of hidden wit that was not apparent at our introduction. He had been flying loads of gear and passengers safely into the Alaskan bush for years and still does today, many more years later. Dave pushed the plane off the beach and fired up his reliable Cessna. Soon we were taxiing out to open water. Then he pushed the throttle to thunderous full power and we started our takeoff. At first the floats grabbed the water like syrup. But within seconds, as we gained speed, the lift created under the wings lightened the floats' burden. White spray flew out to the sides and my heart rate jumped. We were soon skipping over the lake's surface like a racing hydroplane. Then we were airborne.

The ground-level scene disappeared quickly to be replaced by an ever-expanding view of the wild landscape. Multiple lakes, large and small, appeared connected by a web of rivers and streams. I could already see a dozen places where I wanted to toss a fly. Bogs and yellow-green hills of sparse tundra vegetation stretched for miles with jagged snow covered peaks off in the distance.

We wore headphones with mics so we could communicate over the booming engine noise. Egdorf called out the rivers as we flew over; the Tikchik, Wood, King Salmon, Nuyakuk, and many others. We imagined schools of salmon headed up river. Soon afterwards we saw real schools of salmon, schools large enough to be seen from hundreds of feet above. We searched for wildlife and checked off a few of the great Alaskan big game animals in the first hour; moose, caribou and two massive brown bears, their thundering gait and thick slabs of fur-covered muscle obvious even from high above. There was no sign of human activity but game trails crisscrossed the tundra like suburban highways.

We had planned on a few fresh fish dinners during the float and asked Dave Egdorf if he liked the rainbow trout. "Well", he explained through the headsets, "They've been eating rotten salmon flesh for about a month now so here's my favorite recipe. Coat a big frying pan with olive oil and season with onions and garlic. Fry the trout over your fire until the meat begins to flake off the bones. Then throw the trout in the fire and eat the seasoned frying pan." Mike and I had a good laugh and Egdorf's message was clear; we would eat the coho salmon or Dolly Varden instead.

Miles later we approached our destination, the upper Nushagak River. Egdorf made a pass over a long slow run and then circled back around. He descended low heading upstream. Soon we were below the tree tops gliding just feet above the river. The floats made a soft thud as they contacted the water and then skittered over the surface. We decelerated quickly with the aid of the opposing current and, within five seconds or so, the plane became an air boat headed slowly up river. Egdorf steered towards a small eddy. He ran the aluminum floats gently onto the sandy beach and shut down the engine. We had finally arrived.

We quickly unpacked our gear onto the sand and conducted a final inventory. It turned out that Egdorf kept a small gear stash in the forest near our landing beach. Loaded in his Cessna was a box of one-quart oil cans to leave there. "I need to get this motor oil as high up in those trees as I can", explained Egdorf. "If the bears can reach them, they'll drink it all." Damn!

We confirmed and marked our pickup point on the topo map, eight days and 80-miles downriver. Then we helped Egdorf push the floats off the sand and spin the plane 180 degrees to face the river. He jumped back into the pilot's seat and fired up the engine. Dave taxied slowly out into the river and turned down current to gain a speed advantage. With a sudden roar of the engine, the lightly-loaded plane jumped to attention, shot downstream, and was soon lifting off like a kite. The Cessna faded low and to the right and soon disappeared beyond the tree tops.

The adrenaline-charged plane flight and river landing was now suddenly replaced by nearly complete and lonely silence; just the gurgling of the river and soft whoosh of the light breeze. Life, so complex and mechanized in the city, would be replaced for a short time by a simpler, if not safer, world of the river, the fish and the bears. Mike and I were thrilled to be there, almost giddy at times, although a hint of apprehension followed us during our entire stay in the bush.

Our spirits high, we inflated the raft, installed the frame, loaded our gear, rigged our fly rods and shoved off. We each had two rods rigged, an 8-wt. with clear intermediate line for our larger streamer patterns and a second 6-wt. with floating line for drifting egg patterns and flesh flies. We had several more rods packed in their tubes on the raft's floor. We couldn't let a broken fly rod spoil our big adventure.

A gravel bar soon appeared downstream on the inside bend of a promising run. We beached the raft and proceeded with life insurance step number one; securely tying the raft's long bow line to a tree. An unmanned raft lost to the current could be the end of us. Our only survival gear outside of the raft was our waders, jackets, fly rods and a butane lighter I carried in my pocket.

Our primary targets were large leopard rainbow trout and eight-to-sixteen-pound coho salmon. Brightly colored Dolly Varden char, Arctic grayling with their large iridescent dorsal fins, hard fighting chum salmon and even northern pike were also on our list. We fished hard through the first run and picked up a few decent-sized rainbows and Dollys on #4 white Mylar zonkers. The zonkers turned out to be a good all-around searching pattern for every fish that swims in the river.

Remnants of a few dead king and sockeye salmon lay on the gravel bar. These, when counted in the tens of thousands, are the lifeblood of the entire river ecosystem. Nutrients from the Pacific Ocean are carried far upriver in the bodies of the salmon and this feeds, directly or indirectly, every form of life in the valley from tiny lichens to massive moose and the big Alaskan rainbow trout. The pungent odor of rotting salmon flesh always hung in the air at varying intensities. The next river bar was littered with even more salmon carcasses and we were not surprised to see huge bear tracks on the sandy beach.

The best campsites were out in the open on the gravel bars. The benefits were numerous; the breeze away from the alders and spruce kept the swarms of mosquitoes and even more annoying "no seeums" down, handy driftwood was available for fires, and we had quick access to good fishing. The sand and gravel kept our clothing and camping gear out of the mud on rainy days. The biggest benefit of camping out in the open, we figured, was that any bear walking the riverbank at night would be less likely to suddenly stumble upon our tent at close range. There was no use trying to hide from the bears. They are the masters of that environment and it's better to let them know you're around from a good distance. A satisfied bear fattened on salmon was more likely to take a wide path around our camp if it was warned of our presence far in advance. Mike's "Aware Bear" plan included a pee perimeter around camp. Yes, when nature called Mike directed me to strategic locations about 100 feet from our tent to build the human scent advance-warning barrier. With a brown bear's sense of smell being stronger than even a bloodhound, it seemed like a good idea.

The one downside to camping out on the gravel bars was the possibility of exposing the tent to destructive winds if a storm came up, a common occurrence in the Alaskan bush. One night an oncoming storm forced us to move the tent back into the bushy alder trees that grew on the edge of the gravel bar. The bugs were thick back in the trees but at least the tent would stand through the night. The bears are known to like the protection of the thickets as well. We usually walked and fished prospective campsites before unloading the raft. On one promising gravel bar, we discovered a partially eaten caribou calf in a grassy patch just beyond the beach. It had to be a bear kill and we knew how territorial and aggressive a brown bear could be with its food supply. The fishing potential looked good but it wasn't worth the risk so we jumped in the raft and headed down the river.

Most days brought rain showers. Fortunately the heaviest rain usually occurred at night while we stayed fairly dry in the tent. Packing up our wet tent in the morning was never enjoyable, but it became a typical early day activity. We were thankful for a few clear, breezy afternoons when we could dry out our gear and even take a quick icy dip in the river.

When we weren't busy packing gear, unpacking gear, setting up camp, cooking, scrubbing pots and filtering water, we fished nearly non-stop during the long hours of daylight; a major benefit of camping on the river. We counted the near lack of modern conveniences as another benefit; there was little out there to break our 24-7 wilderness trance.

With so many stops at good-looking water, we found it a challenge to make our full ten-mile drift downriver each day; the "drifter's dilemma". Once we left a good fishing spot we couldn't go back; at least not until some year in the future when we could start the entire journey over again. Would the fishing downstream be as good as it is here? Would it be better? We tended to linger on the best runs.

While drifting downstream, the non-rowing angler would sit on the ice chest in the bow, rod in hand, and scan the river for fish. A few surviving king salmon remained from their spawning run two months earlier. Post-spawn king salmon do not live for long. The 30-pound zombies were covered in white fungus and barely able to keep their fins pumping; a sad sight but part of the proper natural ecology on the river. Most of their clan lay dead on the bottom or washed up on the banks. The dead salmon that are carried with the current far downriver all the way to Nushagak Bay are said to be consumed by 200-pound Pacific halibut.

We would occasionally spot small groups of spawning pink salmon and learned that some of the largest rainbows in the river would swim just below the spawning redds waiting for a few salmon eggs to be dislodged. If we saw multiple redds we would beach the raft and tie up. We waded on the clean undulating gravel through clear knee-deep water carefully scanning the bottom for trout. The pink salmon (AKA humpback or humpies) tended to have a few white fungus marks and were fairly easy to spot. The rainbows, even the six and seven pounders, were well camouflaged in olive gray.

I focused intently through the gently flowing water just downstream from each redd searching for the slightest hint of a trout until I was nearly hypnotized. Then, through a brief flat break on the water's rippled surface, I saw a long horizontal shadow. Was that a fin waving? I squinted hard and stared through my polarized lenses. There it was again. I cast my pink egg pattern about fifteen feet above and flicked an upstream mend in the line to remove any tension on the leader. The fly sunk slowly as it gently drifted down, down, down. The fin waved a little faster and the shadow moved a foot to the left. I saw a flash of silver and red as it rolled slightly.

Before I could set the hook the big rainbow was on and shot straight across the run. A dozen salmon spooked and fled. When the super-charged trout reached the far bank in just a few seconds, it leapt into the air almost to my eye level. The fat rainbow landed with a heavy awkward splash and rocketed downstream. I gained line back but was soon met by another powerful run. My drag screamed but the leader held. Fortunately there were none of the downed trees in this run that were common along most of the river.

Eventually the fish tired. A few minutes later, the beautiful trout lay on its side in a few inches of water. Its scarlet flanks and gill plates glistened in the broken sunlight. Hundreds of black spots covered nearly every part of its thick body, a true leopard rainbow. I removed the hook as carefully as my shaking hand would allow and sent the fish on its way home. A day later Mike had a similar experience and landed the largest rainbow of our trip, easily ten pounds!

Evenings in camp were a flurry of work followed by some much-needed physical downtime. I would set up the tent and table while Mike, the better chef, would focus on meal preparation. Dinners of chicken, spaghetti, salmon, chili, potatoes and salad would be considered fairly simple at home but were gourmet fare on the riverbank. It's typical protocol in bear county to keep food and trash far away from the campsite. To some extent we did, but it seemed useless with so many dead salmon carcasses lying around.

Sometimes we would camp near large mounds of sticks and branches over ten-feet tall; beaver dens. As darkness fell, and anytime during the night, angry beavers would swim out into the river and loudly slap their tails on the water's surface, a warning that we were not welcome.

After our long physical days, sleep should have come easily. But it was often disturbed by a gnawing sense of vulnerability. The loaded shotgun lay on the tent floor, but I doubted we would have time to get to it if an angry or over-curious bear suddenly decided to tear through the thin nylon wall of our tent. The gurgling flow just outside usually lulled me to sleep, but I sometimes lay awake and imagined other haunting sounds within the river's song; men talking, a baby crying, bears grunting. At first light one morning Mike asked if I had heard the bear snorting a few hours earlier. "I always hear bears whether they're around or not."

We unzipped the tent door and took a short walk out on the sandy bar. A clear set of new bear tracks moved evenly over the soft ground for more than a hundred feet; but then the tracks went chaotic near our human scent barrier. The impact zones of deep paw craters had thrown loads of sand in random directions. The tracks then turned back into the alders headed away from camp. Mike had heard the real thing.

There were enough tundra-covered hills along the gently meandering river to find our location on the topo maps. The coastal tundra plains leading into Bristol Bay are relatively flat rolling piles of ancient glacial and river deposits; cobble, gravel and sand. The spruce forests are sparse due to the rocky soil, shallow groundwater and short growing season. Occasionally out on the wide-open tundra we would spot caribou grazing. While drifting down river one day, a small herd of about fifteen caribou swam across the river just below our position; quite a sight.

By the fifth day of our journey we had yet to catch or even see a coho (AKA silver) salmon. We may have been too early or above the run moving up from the sea. Finally, later that day, we began to see small groups of big fish headed upriver. They were distinguishable from every other fish we had seen because of their larger size and even more so because of the horizontal black "V" that defined the back edge of their tail fins. Some had a reddish hue.

We pulled over to the inside of a long slow river bend and brought out our heavier 8-wt. rods and reels spooled with clear intermediate lines. The fly of choice was a #1 hot pink bunny leach with streaming red tinsel and weighted barbell eyes. It wasn't long before the action began. We cast across and slightly downstream and let the line swing and the fly sink for about five seconds. Then we stripped the fly back with hard two-foot tugs on the line. The heavy strikes stopped the fly cold, like it had snagged a tree stump. After a split-second delay, the salmon would take off in a sprint downstream, heavier than the rainbows although slightly slower. Much of their battle occurred near the surface with great thrashing and powerful surges; what a fly rod fish! We switched to heavy fifteen-pound Maxima tippet to keep the fights short and to get our flies back out to the next waiting coho. After landing and releasing five or six of the thick fresh salmon, our arms were tired and we were ready to move on.

That night we baked a smaller eight-pound male coho over the fire. Wrapped in foil with butter and lemon, the salmon was delicious. The bones, with considerable pink meat remaining, were tossed into the slow shallow current to cover the scent from the bears. With the last of the day's fading light, I decided to make a few more casts on the long run. I grabbed my 6-wt. rod with the weighted pink and cream flesh fly already attached. I walked downstream for a minute and then began casting and dead-drifting the fly. Several torn-up king salmon carcasses lay on the bottom. We had noticed that some of the largest rainbows came out of hiding in low light to tear at the dead salmon flesh. I worked upstream and approached our camp ten minutes later. I caught sight of our freshly baked salmon remains on the shallow gravel river bottom. And there it was; a huge trout enjoying its best meal of the year! Our gourmet salmon dinner was now being served up to a big rainbow. Did I resist the temptation to drift a fly by the nose of that beast?

Our primordial sensory dials were turned to "High" during the entire river journey. I often paused to make a 360-degree visual scan of our environment and noticed Mike doing the same. Even the slightest sound heard over the constant hum of the river flow stood my hair on end. I wondered if the native Alaskans reacted the same way hundreds and even thousands of years ago.

The following day while rowing through a deep pool, Mike pointed down the river and called out "Bear!" The pool tapered into a narrow run several hundred feet downstream. At its thinnest point, a massive brown bear was feeding on a salmon carcass right at the water's edge.

The bear looked up briefly but then got right back to its meal. I back-rowed to keep our distance while Mike yelled to frighten the bear off the riverbank. It took a few lumbering steps towards the alders but then turned around and returned to its meal. No luck!

After ten minutes of shouting from a safe distance, the bear seemed to lose interest in us. In order to pass we would need to drift within about twenty feet of the bear that must have weighed 500 pounds. Twenty feet was one good leap. A bald eagle circled high above seeming to enjoy our predicament.

We finally lost patience with the stubborn bruin and decided to make a quiet pass, but not before Mike drew the shotgun. I rowed as quietly as possible while Mike leveled the gun. One hundred feet, fifty feet, thirty feet we drifted towards the bear. Then we were even. Our presence barely elicited a grunt. A few seconds later we were safely downstream. I wondered how many other close brown bear encounters we might have had without any clue on our part.

The days passed quickly and the end of our wilderness journey approached. The Nushagak had been just a large stream at the beginning of our journey but was now a full-fledged river, the mighty Nush. The fishing had been good but not easy. Even in this fishing nirvana, we could go many hours with no hookups. But persistence and new water would get us back into fish. On a few quiet mornings we were able to bring coho to the surface with our hot pink skated wogs; the surface wake of the approaching salmon not unlike a torpedo attack. We even caught Arctic grayling one evening on #14 Adams dry flies. On a deep emerald run, Mike hooked two two-foot-long rainbows while swinging a floating deer hair steelhead bomber, their deliberate rises clearly visible to us both.

At noon on our last day we heard the faint mechanical drone of a plane far in the distance; Dave Egdorf! A few minutes later the Cessna passed low overhead heading upstream. Egdorf made a wide turn and passed over us again flying downstream. We lost the sight and sound of the plane around a large bend in the river. Twenty minutes later we rounded the bend and found the Cessna beached a short distance below; our passage back to the "safe" world of modern civilization.

Postscript: The Nushagak River's remarkable wilderness and massive salmon runs of immeasurable value are gravely threatened by the proposed Pebble Mine. Please contact your representatives in Congress to protest this vast open pit mine in the headwaters of the world's most productive salmon habitat.

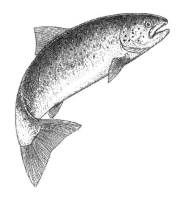

7 BONNIE SCOTLAND

A Strange Pilgrimage to the Birthplace of
Modern Fly Fishing

Ancient forms of fly fishing are described in historical
literature from as early as 200 AD when Roman author
Claudius Aelianus described fishermen wrapping wool and
duck feathers around hooks to catch fish in Macedonia's
Astraeus River. The birth of modern fly fishing as we know
it today is linked to Great Britain in old England and
Scotland. The *Treatyse on Fysshynge with an Angle*
published in London in 1496 describes how to make trout
fishing flies and includes twelve fly patterns. Like much of
old British history, there is some mystery and controversy
regarding the author. Many believe it was written by a nun,
Dame Juliana Berners, although some present-day

111

historians do not agree. If true, this would make Dame Berners the patron saint of fly fishing. Over 150 years later Englishman Izaak Walton published the most famous early sport fishing literary work in 1653, *The Compleat Angler*.

Much of the original modern fly fishing activity was centered in the north of the British Isles in the Scottish Highlands. The Highlands are home to the most legendary fly fishing waters in Great Britain; the Rivers Spey, Tay, Dee and more. Last year a friend invited Mary and me to visit her in Scotland. We set aside two weeks in late August and early September and I began the long and fascinating process of researching the history, most iconic sites, and, of course, the fly fishing potential. For many weeks it involved a six o'clock glass of wine, a large map of Scotland, marking pens and pencils, and the Internet. Mary joined me on many evening planning sessions. The goal was to squeeze the most out of our limited time in Scotland, but also to get us there, at least in spirit, months in advance.

With the wealth of information available on the Internet, it quickly became obvious that we would need far more than two weeks to fit in our itinerary, two years might not be enough. So this first trip would be a mere introduction to be followed up a few years later by a more intimate journey to a few favorite locations. Most of my research focused on the wild Scottish Highlands, basically everything north and west of Glasgow, Sterling and Edinburgh. But these cities were also "must-sees" because of their history and architecture where shops, cathedrals and castles from as old as the Middle Ages (pre-1500s) blend with modern structures and residents. The final plan was somewhat loose. Half our time would be spent in the cities and with our friend Fiona near Glasgow and half would be a driving tour of the Highlands. The planning map was gradually filled in with penciled notes and a yellow highlighter marked a circular tour of the Highlands that intersected the legendary rivers.

I typically order my fishing permits over the Internet ahead of any travel but this is not possible in Scotland unless you book a guide in advance. I hadn't ruled out a day or two of guided salmon fishing but preferred, if possible, to book it on the spot when I knew the unpredictable river conditions were favorable. Fishing rights in Scotland are controlled by the individual landowners and even Scotland's National Parks are mostly privately-held lands. It isn't like North America where a state or provincial fishing permit opens up vast regions of public lakes and rivers to the traveling angler. In Scotland I would need to find the landowner or manager to buy a permit for each section of river or stream. The key was to ask at a local fly shop, pub or inn.

The native sport fish of Scotland, in order of preference, are the mighty Atlantic salmon, sea trout (sea-run brown trout), resident brown trout, grayling and pike. Rainbow trout from the Pacific coast of North America were planted years ago and are also an important sport fish. Salmon are by far the most favored. Their strength, beauty, size and ephemeral migration from out of the cold North Atlantic each year make them the king of all freshwater fly rod species. The legendary Atlantic salmon rivers of Scotland are so revered that they are blessed in formal ceremonies each winter as the first bright "springer" salmon begin to show. Dignitaries speak, performers sing, and then a long line of anglers follow the drone of kilted bagpipers down to the river. A holy cleric blesses the salmon and the water, and a few drams of fine Scotch whisky are sacrificed to the river before the first fly is cast.

Fly fishing for Scottish salmon is as much art and tradition as sport. Since the early 1800s the handcrafting of ornate salmon flies, often from the colorful plumage of exotic birds, has been as much to impress humans as to attract fish. Patterns such as the original Green Highlander, Willie Gunn, Thunder & Lightening and Jock Scott are true works of art. Today many of these intricately-tied Scottish fly patterns spend more time in display frames than they do at the end of a fly line.

Mary and I departed California in late August and, after a few days in Dublin to adjust to our jet lag, made the short flight to Glasgow. Our first stop was the car hire (rental car) counter. The attendant talked us into an upgrade, a sporty little silver sedan, for just a few extra pounds sterling. It turned out to be a good choice on the narrow, winding and often wet roads of the Highlands, while driving on the left-hand side no less. As soon as we left the car lot, and throughout our journey, roadway roundabouts were everywhere taking the place of traffic lights. In urban areas, they were often closely grouped in five, six or seven roundabouts in a two-mile segment. Many were two or even three lanes wide and all entered and exited from the left. Driving through my first dozen roundabouts with white knuckles was less than shaky, but I was able to avoid direct contact with any hard objects. Mary needed similar focus to navigate simultaneously on both her iPhone and the auto's GPS systems that often disagreed. She also added a much-needed second pair of eyes in the roundabouts

Our friend Fiona lives on the shoreline of the Firth of Clyde. The view of the long deep bay from her living room window was framed by green foliage like a large painting that changed every hour with the cloud cover and sun angle. Traditional sail and fishing boats traveled up and down the tranquil bay occasionally interrupted by the conning tower of a Royal Navy nuclear submarine heading out from Her Majesty's Naval Base, Clyde located at the head of the firth and rumored to go back miles into tunnels excavated in the surrounding hills. We enjoyed our introduction to small town Scotland in Rosneath visiting a tiny pharmacy and local grocery market, and chatting with the locals. The old stone chapel and tilted headstones near the village center spoke of the long history of the area.

We visited dramatic Culzean Castle located on a tall coastal bluff near the mouth of the firth. Although it has the requisite cannons and watchtowers, the castle, completed in 1792, appears to be more of a huge country estate than a fortress. Large ornate gardens, lawns and pathways cover the grounds. Stone stables, coach houses and tack rooms formerly supported dozens of horses and carriages. Priceless works of art hang in many of the chambers and seven distinct ghosts are reportedly seen roaming the hallways and stairways at night.

Fiona is a fine chef and treated us to traditional Scottish meals. Her baked salmon and cod with a pastry crust was fantastic. I wasn't as fond of the haggis. This Scottish favorite is a combination of ground sheep innards, oatmeal, suet (sheep fat) and spices boiled in a sheep's stomach. I mixed mine with much larger portions of potatoes. Apparently haggis has an acquired taste that I have not yet acquired.

The first stop on our Highlands driving tour was the city of Dundee on the Firth of Tay, the mouth of the largest river in Scotland. A few miles upriver we found the famous salmon fishing beats at Cargill. Unfortunately, recent heavy rains had elevated the mighty Tay to near flood level and there was no prospect of good salmon fishing for at least a week. We examined the weathered old wooden rest huts along the river, built for anglers and their ghilies (guides).

After a tour of the original golf links and cathedral ruins in St. Andrews in mixed rain and sunshine, we drove towards the River Spey. I was determined to wet a fly line in the Spey which is often considered the epicenter of Scottish fly fishing lore; so famous that an entire style of two-handed rods, casting, flies and fishing techniques are named after the river. The stormy weather had no intention of cooperating with my fishing plans. We wanted to keep our Highlands tour as flexible as possible so we had not reserved any lodging, although we did have a list of lodges along our path that had received good Internet reviews. We ended up spending the night at an inn in the town of Newtonmore on the upper Spey, located in both Cairngorms National Park and the Speyside Region that is world famous for its Scotch whisky distilleries as well as its salmon.

The old inns were a highlight of our Highland's journey with lodging on the upper floors and a pub and restaurant at ground level. Every night the pubs lit up with a loud mixture of locals and tourists, the ubiquitous whisky always playing a role in the festivities. Menus at the pubs listed dozens of Scotch whisky options from the local distilleries, not unlike wine lists at high-end restaurants near the Napa Valley in California.

The pubs didn't always facilitate the interaction of locals and tourists. My search for a fishing permit on the Spey was as challenging and ultimately as enjoyable as I imagined the fishing to be. During a dinner of Mary's favorite roast salmon, and mine Scottish steak pie, we asked the servers about permission to fish the Spey. The word was passed about and soon the innkeeper approached our table. We could find a River Spey fly fishing expert, the innkeeper's brother-in-law, at the end of a long hallway in the "local's bar", a separate pub in the same building. Who would have known? "Ask for Dave", said the innkeeper.

After our fine meal we made the walk down the narrow hallway to find locals who would, hopefully, give me some fishing tips and permit information regarding the Spey that flowed just outside the back door. The local's pub was more casual with posters of Scottish rugby and soccer stars and TV sets tuned to sporting events. We asked the bartender for Dave. He turned and introduced us to an upper middle-aged man sitting solo at the bar wearing worn blue jeans, an old black polo shirt and black cap. "Hi Dave. I'm Dave from California. I hear you're the local fly fishing expert".

"Ye cannae say that but I dae a wee bit of fishing on the Spey. Ye Californians are hard tae understan ye speak sae fast!"

I smiled. Mary and I knew we had met a new friend. Over the next hour Dave proudly told us about life in the Highlands and we understood much of the conversation through his deep Scottish accent. He was an engineer at the inn and the nearby Cairngorms Ski Area. He explained the game of shinty, the ancient stick and ball sport of the early Highlanders similar to field hockey but with aggressive physical contact, some according to the rules and some not. Dave was an officer of the fishing association that managed the upper Spey. We offered to buy a round of Scotch for Dave but he refused and instead poured a few drams of Spey Scotch for Mary and me. He told us about the declining Scottish salmon runs due to overfishing, warmer ocean temperatures, and ocean net pen farming of salmon that gathers waste and disease at the river mouths.

Dave offered to take us to a smaller loch and fish the long rods for brown trout with strings of four or five wet flies, but not until a week later when the weather was expected to improve. Rain pounded on the roof and Dave didn't think there would be much fishing potential the following day. Besides it was Saturday night and salmon fishing is illegal in Scotland on Sundays. "Nae, ye cannae fish for salmons in Scotland on Sundee, but perhaps ye can fine some troot".

At my persistence, Dave came up with a plan. Mary and I could drive up the country road on the bank of the Spey to the small old dam at the outflow of Loch Laggan. The lake's outflow into the upper River Spey should be clear and we might be able to find some local brown trout in the river. Early the next morning I bought my one-day fishing permit at the inn's front desk for nine pounds sterling, the preferred currency in the United Kingdom on the brink of Brexit.

Our drive took us through rugged rolling farm country in the wind and rain. Larger green hillsides and taller rocky bens (Highland mountains) were occasionally visible through the low clouds. Fairytale Highland hairy coos (cows) stared curiously at us as we drove by, seemingly oblivious to the driving rain. A colorful pheasant, the plumage no doubt used on a few traditional salmon fly patterns, crossed the dirt path in front of us. The tires spun in the mud a few times but our rental car, now lacking its original silver luster, moved forward.

This portion of the Spey averaged about 80-feet across and a number of interesting runs, pools, and tailouts formed in the rocky channel. The flow was obviously running high and the water was stained a deep tea brown, but a few feet of visibility remained. I figured I might have a chance, at least between the heavy rain squalls that came through every fifteen minutes or so. We parked near the small dam below Loch Laggan. This was upstream from the main salmon run but a fish ladder had been constructed up the dam's face. On the map the lake was long and narrow, the typical shape of Scotland's lochs (lakes) and firths (bays) that were carved out by ancient glaciers during the last ice age. Water splashed over the top of the dam, driven by gale force winds on the lake's surface. Our position was slightly more protected by the old dam structure and a few large trees on the riverbank.

My trout gear consisted of a six-piece 8-foot 5-wt. rod and my old Orvis Battenkill click pawl trout reel that was appropriately labeled, "Made in England". My jacket and wading gear ~~are~~ waterproof but I could not avoid getting soaked during the few unprotected minutes while suiting up in the pouring rain. Mary wisely stayed in the car exiting for only a few minutes during breaks in the downpour to photograph me fly fishing the legendary River Spey.

I had tied some classic Scottish wet flies, #12 March Brown and Greenwell's Glory, at home before the trip but instead grabbed a trusted #8 olive bead head woolly bugger from my tiny fly box. The pool below the dam entered its tailout through a three-foot-deep bar of slow-flowing water over small boulders, good trout holding water. I began systematically swinging the fly through the water expecting a brown trout to come out of hiding at any moment. I worked up and down the bar in faster and slower, deeper and shallower water. The marabou tail of the bugger looked enticing as it undulated through the run, one of the most effective trout attractors ever. The rain and cold wind continued to swirl around me.

I was confident that I would hook something but I didn't. There must have been trout in this water but I never felt or saw a single sign. I had given it my best effort to no avail. I sat in the car wet and shivering for a few minutes with the heater on its highest setting.

The dark stormy weather set the scene for the next few days. We had passed a number of castles along the way and it now seemed more reasonable to explore ancient castles than to fish. There are hundreds of castles and castle ruins in the Scottish Highlands and their history encompasses much of the history of Scotland. The Highland castles, while not the largest in Great Britain, are some of the most stunning and notorious.

While driving along the River Avon, a tributary of the Spey, we came across a centuries-old stone arch bridge. Mary found a turn-off and we drove down a dirt path to a fairytale scene. A miniature stone castle with a tall turret spire sat beside the ancient bridge. It appeared to be a guardhouse and we almost expected a knight in full dress armor to ride up on his steed at any moment.

The Avon is also a legendary salmon river although recent returns are only a small fraction of the historic runs. We walked down to a pool that I imagined would be perfect salmon holding water in lower flows. I knelt on the wet grassy bank and reached into the water to collect a few shiny white quartz stones to add to our home collection of rocks from beautiful rivers around the world. A few hikers came along and told us that this was a back road into a larger castle, Ballindallich, which we could access by driving a few miles further down the main road.

The mountainous Highlands are naturally spectacular but located in a harsh climatic zone in the North Atlantic Ocean at the same latitude as southern Norway and Sweden. Winters are cold and severe. The cultural history of the

Highlands is as complex as all of Great Britain. Ancient stone circles and burial chambers in modern day Scotland have been dated back to before 8,000 B.C. although no written records of these early Mesolithic nomads (wandering hunters and gatherers) exist. The oldest ruins of stone villages found in Scotland date back to Neolithic settlers thought to have come from Scandinavia around 3,000 B.C.

Celtic people began arriving in the Highlands region from mainland Europe around 900 B.C. Romans attacked and then settled in modern day Scotland in around 80 A.D. naming the region Caledonia. The Romans, however, never fully conquered the Highlands because of the extreme climate and poor rocky soil. A few Viking settlements survived on parts of coastal northern Scotland from the 8th through 15th centuries.

Gaelic Celt settlers gained the firmest foothold in the Scottish Highlands in the 9th century. The population of the mountainous Highlands has always been sparse when compared to warmer and more fertile parts of Europe. Settlers of the Scottish Highlands were rugged, self-reliant and independent. Starvation was a common occurrence up until recent times. As modern governments were established to the south in England, the Highlanders formed loose knit clans, communities that worked together like large family units. Each clan was recognized by its unique tartan, wool cloth woven into colorful horizontal and vertical patterns most commonly seen on the men's kilts.

English society residing a few hundred miles to the south regarded the Highlanders as crude and lawless people.

Many battles broke out over hundreds of years when, among numerous complex issues and claims of royalty, the English Kings tried to tax the land of the clans. Centuries of battles throughout Great Britain created the need for fortified structures to house government leaders, wealthy landowners, their staffs, and military personnel. The castle was born beginning in the 1200s.

The gray stormy weather during our castle tours only enhanced the experience, the sense of mystery and intrigue surrounding the ancient tower spires and thick stone walls. Large elegant dining rooms were decorated with elaborate tapestries, paintings, ceramics and crystal. Heavy rough wooden beams supported the ceilings. Fireplaces warmed nearly every room. Armories were stocked with swords, muskets and intricate suits of armor. Kitchens had big wood-burning ovens with cast iron pots and tables laden with (plastic) bread, suckling pigs and salmon. Stone spiral staircases ascended to the tallest lookout turrets. The cold castle interiors often felt like a maze with numerous entrances, exits and multi-level stairways leading to many of the chambers.

Among our favorites were storybook Ballindallich Castle built on the Avon in 1546 and sinister Eilean Donan Castle originally constructed in the 13th century across the water from the Isle of Skye. Ballindallich is part of a large estate and surrounded by beautiful gardens while more ominous Eilean Donan covers most of a small rocky tidal island. Ballindallich is privately owned and family members vacation in rooms that are off limits to public tours. Sewer pipes now run down the outside stone walls from high above. The original castle toilets, called gardenrobes, were merely open holes that spilled unto the stained castle exterior and any careless bystanders down at ground level. Eilean Donan has been bombarded by invading forces and rebuilt many times over the centuries.

The forbidding ruins of Urquhart Castle built in the 13th century are located on a hill above Loch Ness. During our tour, the clouds parted for a few minutes and we caught some excellent photos of the castle with huge Loch Ness just behind. I made the obligatory visual search of the loch from several vantage points but saw no sign of any strange creatures or disturbances on the lake's surface.

We also explored two of the Scotland's largest and most historic castles just south of the Highlands. The earliest versions of both Edinburgh and Stirling Castles were built in the 12th century. Both were massive forts and walled villages constructed in strategic locations on high rocky bluffs. Stirling Castle overlooks the lower River Forth and the quaintly named Firth of Forth while Edinburgh Castle sits high above the large city center. These castles have been built, rebuilt and expanded numerous times over many centuries as besieging armies bombarded and crushed the heavy stone walls. Imposing iron gates and deep moats secured the entrances to these immense fortresses. Lofty turrets, broad ramparts and dozens of cannons were a formidable, but not always impenetrable, deterrent to invading armies. Legends of Scottish heros William Wallace, Robert the Bruce and others were born here and nearby as they led battles against British invaders.

The Kingdom of Great Britain, the union of England, Wales and Scotland, was established in 1707 but many Highlanders resisted. An army of Jacobites (Scottish Catholics) including many Highlanders won several surprise attacks against the British in 1745. The goal of their uprising was to reinstate exiled Scottish heir to the British throne Charles Stewart (Bonnie Prince Charlie). However, in 1746 the Jacobite forces of an over-confident Prince Charles were brutally defeated by the superior firepower of the British Redcoats on the open battlefield of Culloden Moor near Inverness. Afterwards, the British authorities imposed severe restrictions on the Highlanders outlawing firearms and clan tartans with a violation often punishable by death. Many Scottish Highlanders fled to America where their families were able to exact revenge on the Redcoats 30 years later.

To this day it is unusual to see the flag of Great Britain and the United Kingdom, the Union Jack, in the Highlands. The blue and white St. Andrews Cross of Scotland is flown proudly and often. Military museums in Stirling and Edinburgh Castles depict many of the old battles between Scots and Brits as well as the brave Scottish regiments that fought in World Wars I and II. Pipers in full military dress with colorful tartan kilts play their bagpipes at the castles. The drone of the Great Highland bagpipe symbolizes sorrow and celebration, courage and pride, cheering and weeping. You can feel it in the shrill notes.

We drove back out into the country. The rugged heather-covered glen (valley) above Glencoe holds many fine trout streams and hiking opportunities but the rain poured and the burns (streams) flowed in torrents. Dozens of full waterfalls poured down the high valley walls. Dense Scots pine forests covered less rocky portions of the glen. Red deer occasionally ducked in and out of the trees. We visited the snowless but saturated Glencoe Mountain Ski Resort for a cup of coffee. It reminded me of the early ski areas on Donner Pass in California, owned and managed by dedicated ski club members and not large corporations.

We rarely drove a road in the Highlands that was not adjacent to a stream, river or loch. The scenes of deep green forests, rolling hills and rocky bens visible through breaks in the clouds were striking, but I had to remember to keep my eyes on the road. Narrow and winding, the roads were often wet with flowing rain runoff. Oncoming semi-trucks and tour busses flew by just feet to my right side every few minutes.

There was so much water but so few fishing opportunities. There were trout-filled ponds on the Isle of Skye but the rain fell harder than ever the day we visited. We took the road less traveled around to the southwest corner of the island. The country path narrowed to a single lane high above the crashing Atlantic surf. Recent aerial photos of the coastline had identified the possible former site of a small Viking harbor and we searched for it. At one point a gradual slope of grazing land slipped gently down to the sea. Remnants of straight stone walls ran out into a calmer piece of water protected by a small rocky island just to the northwest. Could this be it?

We finished our tour with a relaxing day trip on the coastal railroad from Edinburgh south to Newcastle, England. The first stop was just south of the Scottish border at Berwickupon-Tweed, England. The small quaint fishing village at the mouth of the River Tweed is historically one of the most prolific salmon rivers in Great Britain. But the river remained high and our time was short so we continued south to Newcastle. The dark castle there (the one on the beer bottle) felt the most sinister of all with its multi-level dungeons.

The sky finally cleared as we rode the train back north to Edinburgh. We arrived back before sunset, in time to walk the Royal Botanic Garden and the Royal Mile, the center of old Edinburgh with some of its most famous architecture from the Middle Ages. I visited a fly shop in a gothic stone building just before it closed at five o'clock. It contained a unique mixture of old and new flies, rods and reels.

We departed Edinburgh for California the following day, a bittersweet end to our first tour of Scotland, the fly fishing trip that wasn't. I didn't catch a fish or even see another angler on the water; a less-than-classic fly fishing journey to a most classic fly fishing and touring destination.

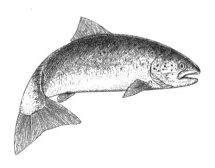

8 EVERYTHING'S A BIT DIFFERENT HERE
Iceland

"Chuck Norris can say Eyjafjnallajokull backwards!" I doubt that it was officially authorized, but it has to be one of the best tourist T-shirts ever. Eyjafjnallajokull is the infamous Icelandic volcano that shut down air traffic to Northern Europe for six days after it erupted in April 2010. On this bright Icelandic morning, however, its gentle snow-capped summit belied its split personality. That's Iceland; strange, unpredictable and beautiful.

Iceland had been on my fly fishing wish list for years, as it apparently has for many other traveling anglers. Internet reports and magazine articles describing the fine salmon and trout fishing in a fantasy landscape have increased dramatically over the years. It took awhile for me to find the right itinerary. I was skeptical of flying in to Reykjavík where I would be rushed to a river lodge and spend five days swinging flies with a guide at my shoulder, only to be rushed back to the airport for my flight home; especially at a price that could exceed US $1,500 per day. I had hoped to spend more time getting to know the Icelandic people and observe the spectacular geology of this unique land.

I finally found a group from Weatherby's Lodge in Maine that was putting together my type of fly fishing journey; two rivers over eight days fishing for both Atlantic salmon and sea trout (sea-run brown trout) with opportunities to catch Arctic char and resident brown trout as well. That is the grand slam of native Icelandic sport fish. The trip included lots of driving around the island with stops at a few of the natural wonders that define Iceland, snow-capped volcanoes, waterfalls, glaciers and hot springs.

I emailed the details to my friend Paul, a veterinary surgeon, world traveler and experienced fly angler living in Oregon. We had fished together on an adventure in Siberia a few years earlier. Paul jumped at the opportunity to fish and explore Iceland. I planned another week after conclusion of the organized fishing to do some additional touring with my wife Mary.

In my usual manner, packing and preparation started far earlier than necessary. I was determined to be organized so that my odds of successful fishing were maximized. But more importantly, all that planning heightened the anticipation. Four months out I was already halfway to Iceland.

I carefully tied dozens of Atlantic salmon and sea trout flies without consideration for the time required, my normal fly tying pace to be truthful. If fly tying had been my profession, I would've starved long ago. Tube flies are popular in Iceland so I bought an adapter for my vice and tied Sunray Shadows, small cone head streamers, the Red Francis with its squid-like tentacle legs, and numerous other colorful patterns both large and small. Most did not and will never get wet, of course, but I didn't want to be caught on the riverbank missing a pattern, color, size or weight of fly I might want. Every one was tied with care. As each fly was removed from the vice I wondered, "Will this be the one?"

The anticipation was finally over and I departed California to rendezvous with Paul in Reykjavik, the modern capital of Iceland. Late into my all-night flight, the airliner crossed the southern tip of Greenland in morning light and I shot some beautiful photos of icebergs and glaciers from my window seat. When I arrived in Iceland, Paul was waiting for me at the airport.

The following morning after sleeping off some jet lag, we took a cross-island flight to Akureyri on the north coast. It was our first in-person glimpse of the bizarre and unique landscape in the remote Icelandic interior. The snow and ice-capped mountains are rounded, relatively flat and extremely broad; primarily shield volcanoes that have erupted over the millennia with highly liquid magma that spread out over the landscape in smooth mounds taking the form of massive warriors' shields laying flat on the earth's surface. Iceland is an active remnant of the separation of the North American and Eurasian continental plates. The resulting wound in the earth's crust allowed magma to leak into the North Atlantic and eventually reach the ocean's surface about 18 million years ago.

This geology and geography created the perfect habitat for the great anadromous salmonids of the North Atlantic, and eventually for fly anglers. From the right-side window seat of the plane, I could see dozens of rivers running down in all directions from the massive icecap of Hofsjokull. I had read about the excellent Atlantic salmon fishing in many of these rivers but couldn't put a name on any of the glistening threads from this high vantage point.

We met the rest of our group at the small airport in Akureyri, a northern Icelandic town located on a deep fiord cut into the sea by ancient glaciers. There we met our guides, Jeff from Maine and Haukur, a native of Iceland. It was a four-hour drive northeast to our first salmon river. Paul and I chose to ride with Haukur in order to gain as much local knowledge as possible.

Our first stop was a grocery store near the regional airport. The store was as clean as the perfectly blue sky outside. The shelves in the mid-sized market were filled with brightly colored food packages from companies I didn't recognize. While Jeff and Haukur filled their carts, Paul and I picked up a few snacks. I felt uncomfortable waiting in the checkout line listening to the young blonde female cashier speak in beautiful, but completely foreign, Icelandic to her customers ahead of me. I didn't really need to speak with her, I said to myself. I could just set my items on the belt and swipe my credit card. It was my turn now and I smiled and blurted out "Hi".

"Well hello. You must be from the U.S." she responded in perfect California-style English.

Shocked I replied with, "Wow, you sound like you grew up in San Diego. How do you do that?"

"We watch a lot of American television. One of my favorite shows is *Friends*. Do you know that one?"

It turns out that all Icelandic students study English in school. That combined with the popular American TV shows means that nearly every Icelander under the age of 70 can make the rapid switch from their native Nordic language to either good or great English.

Our drive to the northeast took us just short of the Arctic Circle. We crossed a dozen rivers and each time I questioned Haukur, "Are there fish in there? What kind?"

Haukur knew each river and had fished many of them. Eventually he began answering my fish questions before they were asked.

The northern Iceland seacoast is similar to what you might find in Canada, Norway or Scotland. The deeper bays and fiords are protected and usually calm, home to several small fishing villages. The points and outer coastline are exposed to the full wrath of North Atlantic storms and mostly uninhabited.

Several fine salmon rivers enter the sea near the town of Thorshofn. We turned onto a sheep ranch just above the town and into the valley of the Hafralonsa. Most salmon rivers in Iceland are located on private ranch land. The fishing rights and management responsibilities are leased to private angling clubs while the government sets the regulations to protect the future of the fisheries.

We unloaded our gear at the simple but comfortable guesthouse and were soon back in the Land Cruiser with Haukur. Our plan for the first afternoon was to survey the upper canyon pools over an hour up the muddy ranch road. The late August flow was dropping and very clear, the clarity being typical of most Icelandic salmon rivers. Much of the snow melting off the ice caps percolates into rocky volcanic soil and emerges further downhill as pure spring water fully filtered during its slow subsurface journey.

After traveling far upriver, we stopped to observe a canyon pool where Haukur expected to find salmon. Looking down from the rim, the deep run varied between crystal sapphire and emerald depending on the water's depth and angle of the sun. Shadows and boulders on the bottom appeared to undulate as soft tongues and ribbons of current flowed over the surface. We squinted and stared intently through our polarized sunglasses while slowly scanning the depths. My water vision came further into focus and there they were, three shadowy meter-long forms gently waving in the flow; Atlantic salmon in their holding run!

It turned out that spotting these fish was easier than hooking them. After a tricky climb down into the canyon, we began casting. Paul and I relied on our North Pacific steelhead experience and gear that isn't much different from the Atlantic salmon anglers' tools. We cast 7-wt. two-handed Spey rods with Skagit lines and MOW tips. By selecting a tip with the proper sink rate, we could, hopefully, swing the fly into a salmon's field of vision.

Haukur stood above where he could observe the relative positions of the moving fly and the holding salmon. The goal was to cast from a position upstream of the fish and slowly sweep the fly from right-to-left a few feet in front of their waiting jaws. One of us would fish while the other would change flies, take photos and look for more fish. Paul gave me the first opportunity and I selected the cone head Red Francis on a #8 double hook, a good traditional fly to begin with.

While standing in the water I couldn't see the salmon finning about 60-feet downstream, but knew their approximate location. After wading into position, I cast my line downstream and across the flow. The fly sank gradually as the soft current began to swing the line downstream. An upstream flip of the long rod's tip reduced the belly, the downstream arc of floating fly line between me and the fly. The mend allowed the fly to sink deeper and slowed the crosscurrent sweep of the fly as it came into the salmon's view. On my first cast, the fly swung too far in front of the lead salmon and it didn't react.

Haukur called out from above, "Another meter of line."

I stripped three feet of line off the reel and repeated my previous cast and swing. Slowly the sunken fly swam down and across the current, hopefully to be stopped in its path by an aggressive, or at least curious, salmon. Atlantic salmon do not feed in fresh water but will strike a brightly colored fly out of territorial aggression, feeding reflex or curiosity; those are the theories. My theory is, since fish don't have hands, they will often use their mouths to inspect an object like we might use our fingers.

The excitement in Haukur's voice grew, "It sees the fly! It's coming for it!"

But the salmon did not strike.

This scenario played out a number of times for Paul and me over the next few days. Late August is towards the end of the salmon run in Iceland. Many of these fish had been in the river for a month or more. A general rule of thumb for salmon and steelhead is that they become less aggressive the longer they've been in fresh water. This seemed to be the situation we were facing. In addition we had warmer and clearer weather than was typical for northeastern Iceland during late summer. While strong sunlight was great for spotting salmon and taking photos of the sparkling river runs, salmon are known to be more wary and less aggressive in bright light conditions.

We made the long bumpy ride back to our guesthouse. The landscape was nearly void of trees, just rocky outcroppings and grasses. A few hearty Icelandic sheep roamed, no doubt enjoying their last easy weather for the year. We could see the bay of Thistilfjordur far in the distance below.

We stopped to examine a few more runs. The salmon we spotted held deep in narrow rocky chutes that would be difficult to fish with a fly. The salmon angling here is designated "Fly Fishing Only, Catch and Release". They are too majestic and too valuable to kill. The old traditions associated with fly angling for Atlantic salmon are revered throughout northern Europe where, hundreds of years ago, modern fly fishing and the art of fly tying had originated in Scotland and England in the pursuit of the noble Atlantic salmon. We never considered harvesting one, but we sure wanted a few up-close photos of living salmon to take back home.

Haukur paused on a hillside and bent over a low tundra-like plant. Blueberries; delicious blueberries! Paul and I joined in the hunt, definitely not catch and release.

Our second fishing day was similar to the first. We saw large salmon in deep crystal runs but I never felt confident about hooking one. The clarity of Iceland's spring-fed salmon rivers is strikingly beautiful but no doubt heightens the insecurity of the salmon holding in those runs.

Several of the deepest canyon runs were impossible to access without climbing semi-permanent ropes hanging down the steep walls. Paul and I examined the hundred-foot lines carefully. While I hate to pass on any fishing opportunity, it didn't seem safe to scale the canyon on those ropes, especially with one hand holding a thirteen-foot fly rod. We decided that our odds of catching salmon were higher if we were alive. Haukur and Jeff climbed down, and back up the ropes the following day.

Paul and I did catch a few smaller brown trout and Arctic char that second day. Haukur mentioned that larger models of eight pounds and more were sometimes caught from the river. A beautiful eight-pound Arctic char fresh from the icy North Atlantic; that would be a prize!

Later in the afternoon Haukur drove us downstream to the lower-gradient section of the river just a few miles above the ocean. The largely gravel bottom was more like the steelhead streams we fished in Northern California and Oregon. The long runs were wider and not as deep as the canyon sections up river; just right for full coverage with the Spey rod. Cast, mend, step once downstream, swing, retrieve. Cast, mend, one step downstream, swing, retrieve. Cast, mend, one step downstream, swing, GRAB!

My first salmon was on and immediately went airborne. This one turned out to be a smaller immature grilse, just over twenty-inches long; but it was an Atlantic salmon. It felt good to touch, photograph and release the fish. Perhaps it was more a sense of relief, a confidence-building moment for sure.

That afternoon Paul and I continued to move up and down a one-mile section of the lower river. It was within walking distance of the guesthouse so Haukur left us on our own and drove two other anglers upstream.

A few hours later the sun hovered just above a grassy ridgeline to the northwest setting slowly at an angle only slightly below horizontal. Paul headed back for dinner while I stayed on the river a while longer. A few minutes later all sunlight was off the water and I sensed the run taking on a different personality. A few new ripples and small waves formed on the pool's tailout. A bonefish guide would call this phenomenon "nervous water", a sign of fish swimming below.

I heard a splash and whipped my head around. A large telltale ring spread out over the surface. I took a few careful steps downstream and scanned the surface. In the growing din a thick fish arched out of the water about 50-feet below my position. I cast and swung the Red Francis through the shallow water. Nothing. I stepped downstream and made another cast hoping to get the swinging fly in the salmon's field of view. The line gradually swung below me. Just as it straightened out directly downstream I saw a soft but definite swirl right where I imagined my fly to be. The Red Francis hung in the current for a second and then I made a short strip. The instantaneous response was a hard grab. Fish on!

The salmon had pounded my fly in knee-deep water and quickly went into maximum escape mode. The heavy fish charged across and slightly upstream. It shot to the surface and made two long low porpoising jumps followed by a deeper run in the same direction. Then it was gone. The long bent rod went straight and my heart sank. It was only a fish, but this one was special, a life fish connected to me for just a few fleeting seconds.

I made a few more half-hearted casts but it was nearly dark and I was sure that the brief commotion had warned any other nearby salmon that their happy hour was over. I waded across the river and walked dejectedly back to the guesthouse. Paul and I ate a quiet dinner. Then it was time to regroup and we strategized over glasses of local Icelandic vodka. The following morning would be our last opportunity for Atlantic salmon on the Hafralonsa.

I awoke early, grabbed a quick cup of coffee and squirmed into my waders. I was ready to go in a few minutes and walked outside to grab my Spey rod off the wooden pegs on the side of the guesthouse. Paul was up and just ten minutes behind me.

A heavy cloud cover blocked the pure blue Icelandic sky from view as I headed down to the river at a determined pace. Fifteen minutes later I arrived at the scene of my thrilling but disappointing encounter the previous evening. I still had the Red Francis fly that had provoked the hard strike the night before and I worked it through the run. Nothing. There was no sign of salmon activity so I waded back to the grassy bank to think the situation over. Paul was just crossing the river a few minutes downstream.

I fingered through my fly box looking for inspiration. A long-time favorite caught my eye, a #8 weighted Prince nymph with tan iridescent rubber legs replacing the normal goose biots at the tail and wings. Definitely not a classic Atlantic salmon fly, the rubber-legged Prince nymph was a top trout pattern and this particular version had saved a few difficult steelhead trips for me. As I tied on the fly, two white Icelandic sheep with long wool coats stared down curiously at me from the hill above.

I moved further up the run into deeper water and began searching with my new fly. This time I used more of a dead drift to get the Prince down where a few salmon from last night's party might be lying. Tension was applied to the fly line only at the end of each drift to raise the nymph and, hopefully, get the full attention of any curious fish that might be following.

At the end of the fifth drift and just as Paul approached, the line went taunt. I lifted the rod tip thinking I might be fast to a submerged rock. But three hard head shakes told me otherwise. Salmon on!

Paul pulled out his camera and I carefully stepped backwards towards the bank with my rod tip raised high as the fish stayed deep and took line in short surges. My pulse jumped. I focused on keeping even tension on the line while not pulling the small hook from the salmon's mouth as I'd done the previous evening. By staying deep and not making chaotic leaps into the air, this salmon gave me better odds.

Ten minutes of give-and-take later, the beautiful hen salmon tired and lay on her side in a few inches of water. I knelt down and cradled her gently as Paul snapped photos. Success! Once the Prince nymph was carefully removed, I held my prize in the slow current until her fins were pumping and she was ready to go. "Thank you and go make babies" I called out as the big salmon swam away.

Paul shook my hand and I thanked him for his diligent camera work. He knew how much I wanted this memory preserved.

We sat on the shoreline grass for a few minutes to celebrate and rest the run while I retied the Prince nymph. "It's your turn now Paul". Sure enough, ten minutes later Paul was fast to another beautiful Atlantic salmon. This time I was glad to be the cameraman. What a morning! One we will always remember.

A few hours later we departed with Haukur for a new river, a long drive through the beautifully bizarre Icelandic countryside. We climbed a well-maintained gravel road to a steep windswept summit and then headed back down towards the ocean far below. Layer upon deep layer of ancient lava formed a giant's staircase down to the sea. Several streams made their descent not far from the road and they fell over dozens of waterfalls in small rocky canyons. Again there was not a tree in sight, just green spongy moss and low-lying shrubs.

We crossed more streams and rivers. Some were ultra clear. Others that flowed directly off the ice fields were colored gray-brown with glacial silt. Haukur called out their names in proper Icelandic dialect.

"Uh, can you pronounce that one again?"

"Hauksstaoahejoi".

I smiled and shook my head in confusion. Haukur responded with a chuckle.

On a remote point high above the sea stood a large metallic orb; some type of radar or communication station. Haukur explained that the USA and Iceland had long been friendly allies. Due to its strategic location, the U.S. military has had a presence in Iceland since WWII. Navy planes could survey the vast North Atlantic for German ships and submarines and, later, Russian subs during the Cold War. With satellite surveillance, the number of U.S. military personnel on the island has now been greatly reduced.

After a petrol stop and mandatory Icelandic hot dog, we arrived in the harbor town of Hofn to spend the night. The contrast between the vast Icelandic wilderness and the modern towns is surprising. Iceland today is on the cutting edge of technology. Wireless Internet and computerized services are common in the population centers. Cell phone service is good and often better in remote locations than in the U.S. Hofn is located near the base of the immense Vatnajokull icecap, the largest in Iceland and larger than any other in Europe. Massive fractured glaciers crawled down from the thick frozen layers above.

The following morning broke with perfect blue skies and cool temperatures. We made a stop at the Jokulsarlon glacier lagoon where huge chunks of calved glacier wait patiently while the tides and slightly warmer seawater slowly work them out through the narrow opening into the surf and sea. The small blue icebergs bobbing out in the surf take on every imaginable shape. Many are deposited by the waves onto the black sand "Diamond Beach" where they amaze visitors while awaiting their slow transformation back to liquid.

Paul and I were ready to get back to fishing, our sore casting shoulders feeling stronger again. We entered another strange landscape with soft spongy moss covering vast lava fields for miles in each direction. It's no wonder that Nordic myths of elves, both good and evil, were inspired here. It wasn't difficult to imagine one peeking out from behind the soft green mounds. The true story was that pure spring water flowed slowly through the porous lava rock just beneath us and would soon reach the surface to form another perfect part-time home for sea-run salmonids.

We turned up another country road and were soon driving along the banks of a wide South Iceland river, the Eldvatn. Imagine a large spring river on the moon. The Eldvatn flows through the lava beds in large slow runs, narrow shoots, and broad shallow tailouts. The migration of large sea trout up from the North Atlantic usually begins in August and it was now early September.

The Eldvatn guesthouse sits alone in a grassy field near the lower river. Most of the best pools and runs are a short drive up dirt and rock roads on either side of the river. Automobiles can cross the river on a bridge located a few miles downstream or through a shallow marked ford for high-centered 4WD vehicles far upstream, a common method of river crossing throughout Iceland. Many of the narrower runs can be fished effectively with a single-handed 8-wt. rod but some of the wider pools and tailouts are more effectively fished with two-handed Spey rods. We pulled up to just such water.

A deep sapphire chute ran at the head of the run and then gradually fanned out into a long broad tailout that averaged about five-feet deep. Long casts would be required to cover a major portion of the most promising flow. We strung up our long rods in the cool bright sunshine. Two-faced volcano Katla loomed in the distance; today and most days a massive but gentle hill blanketed in smooth white snow and ice. But just below the surface, super-heated orange magma under extreme pressure fought to reach the atmosphere above. It had happened before, and in the frame of geologic time, a violent eruption could occur at any second.

Paul and I each made a pass through the promising run allowing our small pink flies to swing through wide deep arcs just above the gravel and grass river bottom. The passes felt right but the bright sunlight was again suspect in our inability to stir any fish activity. We planned to return when conditions improved.

We drove down the riverbank that was mostly uninhabited except for a few old farmhouses. Haukur pointed one out that was abandoned many years ago after a series of mysterious murders marked it as haunted.

That night after dinner, Haukur pulled out a surprise for the anglers at the guesthouse; Viking fermented shark called "Hakarl". Viking explorers from modern-day Norway settled in Iceland in the late 800s A.D. Wood for heating and cooking was scarce so the Vikings developed alternative methods for preparation and preservation of meats. They learned that raw shark meat stored underground and later in a cool dry location for many months would "ferment" allowing it to remain marginally edible for long periods of time. The accumulation of ammonia during the fermentation process kills off microorganisms that would decay the flesh but leaves the meat with a strong aroma and flavor, to say the least. Today, you can buy Viking fermented shark in small plastic tubs in Icelandic grocery stores.

We tested the Hakarl in very small chunks. Those who had success did not inhale until the chewy morsel was swallowed. A quick shot of Icelandic vodka helped to keep the ultra-pungent morsel down. One of our fellow anglers likened it to canned tuna that had been left open in the refrigerator for six months. I joked that it should not be eaten until it had aged far beyond the expiration date on the container. Those Vikings were tough. As we continued this great Icelandic tradition, the vodka became much more popular than the fermented shark. Our celebration was suddenly interrupted, "Come outside, quickly!"

I shot out to the wooden deck under a sea of stars. A faint glow crossed the sky like a weak search light beam. Within a few seconds though, the beam flashed bright florescent green as if a switch had been flipped. The Northern Lights! The intensity brightened and the beam began to wave like a heavenly banner in a gentle breeze. Flashes appeared here and there like a slow motion fireworks display. The dazzling light show went on for ten minutes. Then, as fast as it appeared, the stunning Aurora Borealis was gone…but forever imbedded in my memory.

We returned to our promising run the next morning under cloud cover and light rain. The two-handed Spey rods came out again and I tied on one of Haukur's own Skotta patterns. (Skotta: a female ghost in Icelandic folklore). The rhythmic searching began with the double Spey cast for right-handed casters fishing from river right.

The double Spey is executed in a series of continuous steps: the setup with the rod tip pointing upstream and about 30 feet of line and leader hanging downstream; the low horizontal sweep of the rod from left-to-right; the formation of the large horizontal "D" loop behind the right shoulder; the overhand forward cast stopped hard at ten o'clock and the final release of running line looped under the index finger. All of this occurs in about three seconds and, if the timing is correct, the line loops and sails far out over the river.

A good Spey cast is a reward in itself and, in my experience, no harder to learn than the single-handed double-haul cast. Just as in all sporting endeavors, the Spey casting practitioner will have good casting days and middling days. The wind strength and direction are important factors and so are the weight and bulk of the fly. But even on a mediocre day, the double-handed Spey cast will shoot the fly out over 80 feet without the fatigue of single-handed casting. This can be of major muscular benefit when casting 500-600 times each day for multiple consecutive days.

The hypnotic rhythm of cast, mend, step, swing, retrieve and repeat soon had my mind wandering in a fuzzy state of consciousness; part of the artistic allure of Spey casting. The cold waist-deep water rocked me gently. Cast, mend, step, swing, retrieve. Cast, mend, step, swing, retrieve. Repeat and repeat again.

Fifteen minutes into my daydream, the bowed fly line sweeping downriver suddenly tightened. Fish on! The strong silver sea trout swam quickly to the surface followed by a low heavy jump, not as high nor as graceful as the Atlantic salmon but impressive nonetheless. The thick sea trout dove deep and began the bulldog routine that its all-freshwater brown trout relatives are famous for. Short powerful bursts soon had the line out into the backing. Ten minutes of give-and-take later, the big buck was swimming near the bank and I led him into a small shoreline spring. This was a fantastic Icelandic specimen of perhaps sixteen pounds!

Paul and I worked hard for a couple more nice fish from the same run. Later that afternoon Haukur pointed out an interesting phenomenon along parts of the lava-covered shoreline. "Icelandic drinking fountains" were small mounds of pure natural spring water gurgling up from the ground. Tiny cracks in the impervious rock cover allowed pressurized groundwater from below to rise to the surface; nature's version of a leaking water pipe. We knelt down and sipped on the miniature Icelandic water fountains; pure, cool, perfect water.

We fished until dark that evening and watched a few big sea trout roll in our favorite run. In my experience, there is a very short list of "perfect" river runs that I've fished over the years; long gradually bending flows with great holding water and current that presents the fly enticingly to the fish. I know one on the Rogue River in Oregon, one on Slough Creek in Yellowstone (not where you think), one on a remote river in Siberia that Paul and I had fished, one on the Rio Tic Toc in Chile that I will probably never reach again, two on the Morice River in B.C. and precious few others. I added this run to that special list.

We drove back to the guesthouse that evening in the dark. I swear I could see a dim light through the window of the haunted farmhouse. Haukur told us the Icelandic legend of the Huldufólk, the hidden people that can appear and disappear at will. Sometimes half-human and half-goat, these ancient and often evil mythological creatures roam the Icelandic countryside in two parallel worlds. Many Icelanders still believe.

Our final fishing day came and we picked up another nice sea trout. Like the others it was carefully landed and released; held just above the river for a few seconds to be photographed as water drops rolled off its fins.

Paul (braver than I was) decided that we should check out the haunted farmhouse before we departed the river. It was not as ominous under the bright sun, but I hesitated nonetheless. We parked on the grass nearby and, with Paul's encouragement, slowly approached on foot. The old wooden structure was two stories tall, actually one-and-a-half stories since the lower floor was barely five-feet high. Soil and thick grass sloped up the exterior walls to the eaves and thinner sod covered the roof. Only the front door and one upstairs window were uncovered.

Paul ducked down and entered the low front doorway while I tentatively peered into the dark room. The air was musty and damp like a subterranean cave. The floor was compacted dirt. A strange animal skull was nailed to a weathered gray post just inside the entrance; a warning no doubt.

The bottom floor appeared to have been a stable for goats and other farm animals. Apparently this was the traditional Icelandic practice for keeping farm animals alive and farmers' families warm during the long, cold, snowy and dark winters. The stench in the upstairs living quarters must have been horrendous. Today, clean winter heat is no longer a problem in Iceland with the abundance of hydroelectric and geothermal energy.

Paul walked up the narrow rickety wooden staircase while I crawled up the exterior soil slope and peered through the single window. The dusty bare-wood living area was nearly empty. The only sign of activity was one perfectly folded wool blanket laid out on a wooden bed frame. I shivered at the eerie sight. We each shot a few photos to document our strange visit. To the best of our knowledge, neither of us have been visited by the Huldufólk since our brief tour of the haunted farmhouse.

A day later I was back at the Reykjavík Airport to say goodbye to Paul and welcome Mary. We spent a few days in the city checking out the spectacular cathedral tower of Hallgrimskirkja, the quaint streets, and the statue of Leif Ericson, the Icelandic hero and first known European to set foot on North American soil. The local seafood was excellent and, surprisingly, several Thai restaurants served the same delicious Asian food that we find in California. Most Icelanders can trace their Nordic family roots back many generations within their home country; but some Thailand natives have apparently immigrated to Iceland more recently and brought their excellent culinary skills and recipes with them.

Mary and I visited South Iceland and lingered at a few spots that Paul, Haukur, Jeff and I had hurried by in our rush to reach the rivers. We stayed in a beautiful inn on an Icelandic horse and goat farm near Hvolsvollur for a few days. We visited the spectacular waterfall of Skogafoss and the tall thin veil of Seljalandsfoss with a slippery green trail that leads behind the falls. We toured the active geyser field and photographed the original "Geysir" that is now dormant. We made it back to the Jokulsarlon glacier lagoon and Diamond Beach where Mary raced out to touch the grounded blue ice sculptures between waves. We drove along the southern coast where tall green lava cliffs rise in the fashion of Hawaii's Kauai, except where the occasional glacier pokes through.

We felt the power of Iceland's two-layer version of Niagara Falls, Gullfoss. We drove the shores of Lake Thingvellir located in the rift zone between the two continental plates. The lake holds an ancient strain of the world's most beautiful land-locked brown trout with distinctive dark markings and irredentist blue cheeks. Some grow to a weight of over twenty pounds. I drove by without a cast.

We woke up several times each clear night to look for the Aurora, but it did not make a second showing. We're planning another trip to Iceland to catch one of the wondrous Aurora Borealis displays and a Thingvellir brown trout.

9 CALIFORNIA GOLD
Sierra Nevada

Rumors run wild in the search for Sierra Nevada Golden trout. The truth is usually hidden beneath a blanket of silence like an alpine stream under winter ice.

Rock Creek Lake in California's eastern Sierra Nevada range is a high-altitude gem that you can drive to in summer. The sapphire blue lake sits at an elevation of 9,600 feet and is surrounded by castle-like granite peaks that reach up another 4,000 feet into the clouds. My family and friends have enjoyed years of great camping, hiking, and fishing in this outdoor wonderland.

The old Rock Creek Lake Resort store and cafe on the east end of the lake is the type that I always loved as a kid. The shelves are loaded with canned chili, mac & cheese, Hershey's chocolate bars, spaghetti sauce, marshmallows and Coleman fuel. A while back I paid another visit, as much for nostalgia as the need for supplies. The wood-framed screen door springs creaked out a greeting as I entered, followed by a sharp "whack" as the door slammed shut behind me. As always, I was quickly drawn to the small store's large fishing section with all its brightly colored lures and trout flies.

A cork bulletin board on the wall was jam-packed with curled and overlapping fish photos hung on straight pins. Proud anglers held their catches of stocked rainbow trout from the lake. One photo, though, was much different and caught my full attention. Half of the photo showed a horizontal slab of granite. The other part glistened with emerald water so clear that it could have been a tropical coral reef. A sheer cliff rose from the lake's far side. Most striking, though, were the two large golden trout lying on the granite slab. They appeared to be nearly twenty-inches long with the unmistakable bright orange and scarlet markings of the High Sierra golden trout.

My curiosity was fully engaged, "Where did these remarkable trout came from?" Hand-written in pen along the bottom edge of the photo was a clue, "Rock Creek Backcountry". That was enough to set me on my own wild gold chase.

I had caught golden trout before, especially during the two summers I worked as a biology field tech in Sequoia National Park. Four of us working in two groups of two had the enviable task of backpacking into remote high-altitude lakes and conducting trout species and population surveys. For a twenty-something year old that loved trout and high mountain country it was a dream job. I was paid but would have gladly done it for free.

Sequoia National Park is named after the world's largest trees and is also home to the highest peak in the Lower 48, Mount Whitney. All of the hundreds of rockbound, high-altitude lakes in the Sequoia region were fishless until stocking by mule train commenced when the park was established in 1890. Aerial planting of fingerling rainbow, golden and brook trout (char), eventually replaced the pack mules hauling milk cans until the National Park Service ceased all trout-stocking operations in the 1970s. Roughly half of the park lakes and two thirds of the streams have self-sustaining trout populations today.

In some of the highest lakes we surveyed, a few over 11,000 feet in elevation, we caught golden trout. These golden trout populations had been transplanted a few miles north from their native creeks in the upper Kern River basin. Originally, there were no golden trout in any lake until they were transplanted by well-wishing humans. With their large parr marks, scarlet and orange flanks, and yellow-gold accents, the gorgeous golden trout is a sight to behold.

Back to that photo; the day after I returned home from Rock Creek Lake, I drove to my local REI store and picked up a few USGS topographic maps for the region that I considered "Rock Creek Backcountry". Those maps lived on my dining room table for a few weeks (fortunately my wife knew about these characteristics of mine before we married). My work at Sequoia had taught me a few things about the lakes that would sustain golden trout populations. The preferred lake elevations are 9,500 to 11,500 feet. At that altitude some snowfields never melt. The larger and deeper lakes are more likely to hold golden trout, probably because they never freeze solid during the long winters, even in those years when the snow pack exceeds a depth of twenty feet.

I searched the maps for lakes with green patches near the shoreline, meadows that would supply ants and grasshoppers for the trout when the afternoon winds of summer blow during the short growing season. Another important consideration was spawning habitat with moving water that could be accessed by mature goldens (some only six-inches long) from the lake.

Golden trout, like their close relative the rainbow trout, spawn in spring conditions, which at high altitude may not occur until summer. Any short section of snowmelt stream with fine gravel is usually adequate. Sometimes a small waterfall cascading onto a shallow gravel bar in a lake is sufficient for spawning. Unfortunately, the condition of those small streams and waterfalls was not evident on the USGS maps. Google Earth can sometimes be helpful but the resolution in my backcountry region of interest was too low to make out sufficient detail.

I knew that most of the golden trout lakes are not found along the main trails, although there are some exceptions. You can get into the vicinity hiking the John Muir Trail or other backpacker highway, but most of the best golden trout lakes sit in high alpine cirques, bowls cut out of the granite by ancient glaciers. Reaching these lakes often requires a scramble of a few miles off the main trails and a climb of several thousand vertical feet over steep rocky terrain far above the timberline. This is some of the world's most spectacular scenery, not unlike the Swiss Alps. Your eyes and camera always love the visions of knife-edged peaks and deep blue lakes; your lungs, blistered feet, and aching legs, not so much.

The search for gold in the "Rock Creek Backcountry" was narrowed down to four lakes. All are accessible, at least marginally, from the Little Lakes Valley trailhead at Mosquito Flats above Rock Creek Lake. The paved parking lot lies at an elevation above 10,000 feet. On the drive up, vehicles cough and sputter giving you a taste of what's in store for your body. To access even one of those lakes above the Little Lakes Valley would be a major effort, so I set out to refine my search. I made smaller color copies of the maps and carried them with me for a few years during my fly fishing road trips to the eastern Sierra.

There is an unmistakable mystique about golden trout in the California mountain towns of Lone Pine, Independence, Bishop and Mammoth Lakes. These small communities are located along US Hwy. 395 as it winds north to south sometimes 10,000-feet below towering granite summits only a few miles to the west. I attempted to get some information when I visited the fishing tackle stores in those towns. But when I pulled out the maps and pointed to my suspect lakes, the shop employees often responded with "maybe" or "I'm not sure about that one". I tried to read their eyes and sometimes thought I might be getting a little closer to solving the puzzle.

Golden trout anglers in the eastern Sierra Nevada are secretive and often come from the ranks of local rock climbers, skiers, snowboarders, mountaineers, trail runners and mountain bikers. Some are endurance athletes that can leave the trailhead solo at 4 AM and return at 7 PM with a month's full of golden fishing memories from one high-calorie day (I suspected that the Rock Creek Lake store photo came from one of them). Most golden trout anglers, like me, are just regular human backpackers that will spend a week in the high country to get one or two short sessions in golden trout heaven. The locations of the golden trout fraternity's secret lakes are held tightly. The prevailing attitude is that loose lips can destroy a remote and pristine fishery.

Rumors of golden trout likely started in the mid-1800s when hardy gold prospectors searching for the next Mother Lode are believed to have discovered isolated populations in the upper Kern River Basin. Those miners, with their focus on gold, likely named this uniquely beautiful trout. The scientific name *Oncorhynchus mykiss aquabonita* came later.

The legend of California's golden trout was enhanced in the 1940s when a few Japanese Americans held captive at the Manzanar Internment Camp (ironically located near Independence) snuck out and headed west into the steep Sierra canyons. The allure of the glowing sunrise on towering granite crags must have been too strong to resist. The prisoners climbed high and found golden trout. I can't imagine the contrast, the sense of freedom they must have experienced up in the high country. A rare black and white photo of Heihachi Ishikaea displayed at the Manzanar Historical Museum shows him with a stringer full of golden trout. It would not be surprising to learn that he guided a few of the camp guards up to these alpine lakes on future fishing trips.

The following August I backpacked into Little Lakes Valley with my family. About four miles in we set up base camp near the shore of an odd-shaped rocky lake above 10,000-feet in elevation. This is the zone where just a few twisted foxtail pines survive the long brutal winters. Summer days are usually warm but nighttime temperatures often fall below freezing. My sixteen-year-old son Michael and I planned day climbs into two of the possible golden trout lakes. After a day of acclimatization, we set out to the easier of the two. Apparently it was too easy. There were no goldens but we did land some healthy rainbows up to a foot long.

The next morning we woke at first light and fired up the little MSR stove for the usual breakfast of oatmeal, raisins and almonds. I loaded my daypack with nuts, cheese sticks, granola bars, maps, a first aid kit, knife, long underwear, and two light space blankets. An injury requiring an overnight stay at that elevation without a sleeping bag could be your last and there is no wood up there to build a fire. That accounted for the long underwear and space blankets. My fly fishing gear was minimal and included a small reel with 4-wt. floating line, a small box of flies, spare leader and tippet, and my cherished five-piece fiberglass trout rod that I had built many years before. Michael carried a similar outfit.

We headed up the trail for a mile to a group of small lakes at the head of the valley and then climbed the only accessible route to the rim. After an hour of steep climbing, some hand-over-hand, we entered a high nearly treeless plateau with several lakes. The thin air at nearly 12,000 feet left my chest pounding and head fuzzy, but didn't seem to faze Michael who had spent the past two months in conditioning for the upcoming high school football season. The dark blue lakes and white snowfields contrasted sharply against the rocky lunar landscape.

We had fished the larger and lowest of the lakes a year earlier and caught some decent brookies, but no goldens. After a short break we hiked another hour up a glaciated granite staircase to the upper lake. We set up the fly rods and tied on my go-to high lake rig, a #10 foam grasshopper with a #18 bead head tiger midge on a two-foot dropper. The primary food sources for these high altitude trout, when they're not eating smaller trout, are hoppers, ants, mosquitoes and other midges so this basic rig usually gets their attention.

We walked and sometimes climbed the rocky shoreline casting over eerie submerged ledges that disappeared into the cold depths. The early afternoon wind had begun to blow and the lake's crystal surface started to dance with the cool breeze. Suddenly, from the deep, a dark missile shot up from the shadows. It stopped and hovered a few inches below my hopper, seemingly in midair. The slight surface chop must have been just enough to hide my imitation's true identity because a second later it splashed on my fly. Fish on!

This one wasn't huge, a foot long at best, but it was healthy and strong. As I brought it towards me its bright red-orange belly flashed. Golden! I snapped a quick photo and send it on its way. We hooked a few more, all eight-to-twelve-inches long. While any golden trout makes for a fantastic fishing experience, I knew this was not the lake in the photo. It was a great adventure with Michael but not quite the Mother Lode.

On our way out a few days later we stopped again at the old Rock Creek Lake Resort for some of their famous "Pie in the Sky". The photo was no longer pinned on the wall but I asked our young server about it. He remembered the picture and knew the angler that climbed into the high country, but was hesitant to give me the lake's name. Armed with my new information, I pulled out my map and pointed to my new number one suspect. The waiter looked uncomfortable but nodded feebly. Found it!

The only consistent window for successfully climbing to the highest Sierra Nevada lakes is August. Even then, there are snowfields to cross and climb, remnants from the deep winter snowpack. The first week of August the following summer would be the week before Michael started football practice, so that's when we'd go. My long-time fishing buddy Steve was getting into backpacking and wanted to catch his first golden trout. He was excited to hear that the big trout lake had likely been found. Steve was in for the following August. We had our team, Steve, Michael and me. Three is good team number for traveling off-trail in the remote High Sierra because it allows one to stay and one to go for help if the third member is injured and must remain on the mountainside.

We had plenty of time to plan and our enthusiasm grew each month. Steve and I started by looking for the safest and less strenuous route to the lake. Reviews of topo maps showed that there was no easy way in. The eagle's-eye view from Google Earth was incredible but daunting with all of the steep rocky alpine terrain that we would need to cover, twice in one day. We could get into range on existing trails, but the last four miles would be over loose talus passes, smooth glaciated slopes and high elevation snowfields. It appeared too treacherous to carry full backpacks for an overnight stay.

We decided to set up a base camp and then climb and fish the remote golden trout lake in one long hard day. We planned to backpack high into the Little Lakes Valley and set up camp. After a day to rest and acclimate to the elevation, we would leave our tent and warm sleeping bags behind for one extended day from dark to dark.

Fitness would be key and we each had a plan; Steve trained hard at home with P90X, I added extra hours at my local gym while Michael just had to keep up with his normal high school sports workouts. The climb in would be long and difficult and any rest time would be subtracted from our one limited fishing session.

August came quickly and we made the long drive up to Rock Creek Lake and then to Mosquito Flats. Along with our golden trout team we had a great base camp crew of our wives and my youngest son Adam. The five-mile hike into base camp on a beautiful alpine lake, right at the timberline, went well although there were plenty of thumping lungs and tired legs. We set up camp on a near-perfect natural campsite. The early-summer outflow from the lake left a flat dry ephemeral streamed of fine decomposed granite, ideal for setting up the tents. A melt pond a few hundred feet downstream warmed up enough under the midday summer sun to serve as a bathing pool. The twisted red trunk of a lone foxtail pine, a rare survivor of the harsh winters at an altitude of nearly 11,000 feet, made a good leaning post for backpacks and a great foreground subject for photos of the saw-tooth peaks towering above. A glacially-smoothed granite outcropping with a few stunted shade pines was a fine kitchen. On the lakeshore, a small patch of grass fringed with yellow wildflowers was our dinning and reading area. Young Adam, a golden trout fisherman in training, cast a small spinner and landed a few rainbows close to camp.

We spent the next day organizing our small daypacks and fishing gear for the big climb coming up. Again we packed long underwear, space blankets, topo maps, a first aid kit, cheese sticks and granola bars. To save a few ounces we left our water filter at camp and brought along a few tiny iodine water purification tablets for our water bottles. The chance of contracting Giardia from the high alpine water sources is low although a few mammals that can carry the protozoan, mainly marmots and pika, thrive at those elevations eating summer grass and hibernating under the winter snowpack in rocky crevices. Our fly boxes were also tiny with just a few small foam grasshoppers, Adams and midge emerger dry flies, and small bead head zebra and tiger midge nymphs.

My wristwatch alarm beeped at 4:30 AM and soon our sleepy but excited team was sitting on the grass around the tiny one-burner stove, headlamps on, as the first glow of morning sun peaked over the eastern ridgeline. Strong coffee came first followed by extra oatmeal and handfuls of nuts. It was time to head out. The first mile was hiked in low light along a trail that we had traveled many times before. The trail ended and we climbed up towards our first plateau, sometimes hand-over-hand. An hour later we crested into the same basin where Michael and I had caught the smaller golden trout the previous summer. This was the first of three ascents required to reach the high pass above our ultimate destination.

A thirty-minute walk along a relatively flat glacier-scoured ridge nearly allowed us to catch our breath. The next climb was more daunting because of the piles of car-sized boulders littering the steep slope. Traversing a half-mile took over an hour, each movement requiring concentration to prevent falling between the large rocks. Sometimes we jumped to the next boulder. Other times we crawled in a zigzag course. We stayed close but each of us picked our own route through the rocky maze. Fatigue was becoming an issue but the draw of the big golden trout was stronger and we moved upward.

We reached the next plateau and were greeted by a spectacular sapphire blue alpine lake, ringed by jagged cathedral peaks without a tree in sight. It looked like a perfect golden trout lake with one exception; this cirque faced towards the north. In my experience, the south and east-facing lakes were more likely to hold goldens, likely because the summer sun shone more directly while the north-facing cirques were in shade most of the day. The short growing season in the highest lakes requires every ray of sunshine. Steve shot some outstanding photos while Michael and I refilled the water bottles and dropped a tiny iodine tablet into each.

The hike and climb up to the lake held us at the edge of our physical stamina for hours. A moderate and steady pace moved us towards our high-altitude goal more efficiently than quicker spurts with frequent rests. The rest breaks, while sitting on a rock and taking in the surrounding peaks, were not a problem; it was the restarts that were tough. Those dizzy and nauseating first fifteen minutes after each rest break reminded my legs and lungs to strain and complain. Eventually my screaming legs gave into my will and the scream was reduced to a numb whisper, or later in the climb, a loud conversation. Steve and Michael seemed to be having the same experience.

The final rocky pass above our destination was now in sight. The steep terrain was half snowfield and half loose talus. We alternated between slippery snow and broken rock that would slide half a step downward for each strenuous step upward. The snow was beginning to soften and, as we advanced, it became easier to kick in steps and stay off the loose rocks. Twenty minutes later we stood there giving each another high fives. The late morning sun felt warm even at an altitude of nearly 13,000 feet.

Our goal was now in sight and not just as a blue splotch on a topo map. The large lake was a thousand feet below the pass, accessible over a long talus slope. We had to descend the southeast face and it held no snow. Giving in to the excitement, we slid and hopped downhill too fast to insure the safety of our ankles and knees. I jogged across the final meadow down to a shallow rocky cove and strung my rod as fast as my shaking hands would allow. The first cast was attacked by a golden about a foot long. As I reeled it towards the bank I turned to see Steve and Michael rigging up.

We moved to a deeper area that looked more like the scene in the photo. Only half of the lake's shoreline was even accessible due to the steep cliffs and huge boulders. Within thirty minutes, we had each landed and released nice golden trout up to sixteen-inches long, the first for Steve. The sense of desolation in that deep rock-bound cirque was intense. There wasn't a single sign of any previous human activity, not even a gum wrapper.

The frigid water was so transparent that we could clearly see every trout rise up to our flies from the depths. Our first few fish were caught from near shore above submerged boulders. When those golden trout became more wary we cast our flies blindly far out into the lake and waited. The sight of a floating yellow grasshopper above must be the ultimate enticement for a hungry golden trout.

Suddenly a big shadow moved quickly up towards Steve's grasshopper lying forty-feet out from shore. It hesitated for a few seconds and then struck the fly. Fish on! The big golden thrashed on the surface and then ran. It looked like the twenty inchers in the photo but unfortunately stayed hooked for less than ten seconds. The one downside to foam hoppers, with their splayed legs, is their inconsistency in solidly hooking trout.

Our initial excitement was gradually replaced by a gnawing anxiety. Our tired legs would need to carry us back over the same route that we had followed in. The long grueling day allowed us only two hours of fishing time. One more large golden rose to my fly. It hovered briefly just below the yellow hopper while my striking hand quivered around the cork. But then it sank back into the depths. It was time to leave the Mother Lode.

Our exhausted bodies hauled us slowly up to the pass. At least from there it was all downhill back to basecamp. We sat and slid down any snowfield we could access even if it took us a little off our path. Our strained knees and ankles continued to move us downhill while our tired lungs took a well-deserved break. Gravity did most of the work but each step required concentration to avoid falling in the chaotic jumbles of granite. Three hours later we straggled into camp to a warm welcome, warm dinner and warm sleeping bags.

Postscript: Parts of this story were written while sitting on the banks of Golden Trout Creek and while in my tent above the creek's meadow to avoid the evening mosquitoes. Golden Trout Creek, tributary Volcano Creek, and adjacent South Fork Kern River are the original habitat of the golden trout and located in California's Golden Trout National Wilderness.

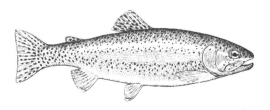

10 KIWI STYLE

New Zealand with a side trip to Fiji

Food poisoning was no way to start a long-awaited adventure. It wasn't from an exotic jungle meal or raw seafood. It must have been the club sandwich at LAX before we boarded our flight. The thought flashed through my mind as my eyes popped opened and I began a desperate ten-second scramble from my window seat to the tiny airline bathroom stall.

My wife Mary and I were four hours into our flight from Los Angeles to Nadi, Fiji on leg one of a fly fishing and sight-seeing trip to New Zealand. Since our trans-Pacific flight refueled in Fiji, we decided to check out the islands for a few days. Without going into detail, the second half of the flight and long shuttle ride to Viti Levu's Coral Coast was excruciating; no way to be introduced to a South Pacific paradise.

As the sun rose the next morning I caught a window glimpse of the white sand beach fringed in swaying coconut palms and the coral reef just a short swim offshore. Sadly my mind and body were in no condition to appreciate the storybook South Seas surroundings right outside. Mary, always quick to make new friends, had met a nice couple from Texas on our shuttle ride and I encouraged her to go out and explore with them. They headed out down the beach towards a local village. That left me to wait out the nausea, headache and dizziness.

After a few hours, my boredom became stronger than the nausea. The tropical scene called me outside to take a swim on the reef. I grabbed my fins, snorkel, and mask and took the short walk to the water, still dizzy and weak. The large natural tidal pools near the beach were protected by a larger coral reef on the outside. The water was like a warm tropical aquarium. As I floated in the clear soothing water, I learned a lesson in human physiology; within ten minutes all my food poisoning symptoms were gone. Apparently the 80-degree water cooled my body temperature enough to eliminate the fever. Needless to say, snorkeling was my chosen activity over the next few hours.

Hundreds of brightly colored tropical fish swam in and out of the fan and staghorn coral; angelfish, squirrelfish, parrotfish and many others. A few larger predator fish circled further out, needlefish and small trevally. The sight of the larger fish through my mask made me wonder if there might be some fly fishing potential. As I began swimming back to shore, I looked towards the beach to see Mary waving.

She was excited to tell me about her day. After a long walk down the beach road, Mary and her Texas friends came to a quaint native Fijian village. There wasn't much activity but they could hear singing coming from the open windows of one of the larger buildings. It was a church and it was Easter Sunday. They walked up to the open door to look in and a tall dark man smiled and motioned them to come inside. Mary and friends sat in a rear pew and listened to beautiful harmonies and a powerful sermon, all in a language they could not understand.

Afterwards, a few of the women wearing long flowery dresses walked over to greet them. One spoke English and Mary made a new friend. Coincidentally, her name was Maari. She gave Mary and the Texans a tour of the village. Maari owned a small store that was, of course, closed on Sundays but she invited Mary and her recovering husband back the next day.

Mary joined me to snorkel over the coral and tropical fish for a few hours and then we headed back to our room. I felt well enough to join her for an early dinner although my meal was just a banana and a beer. After dinner I grabbed my fly rod and we walked along the beach as the sun sank low towards the horizon. We kept our eyes on the water, Mary hoping to see the "green flash", the moment the sun dipped under the surface of the South Pacific Ocean and me hoping to see signs of active predator fish.

I waded in and cast a small blue-and-white popper around the shallow reef structure where I had seen a few larger fish while I was snorkeling. This was just a trial run but I did have a few swirls behind the chugging surface plug. Nothing stuck. During our walk back just before dark, we watched the eerie silhouettes of large fruit bats fly from tree to tree.

The following morning I woke before first light feeling almost normal. Mary slept in while I headed back to the inner reef with my 8-wt. fly rod, the heaviest I had since this was mainly a trout fishing trip. The light South Pacific breeze was already warm even before the sun rose over the flowered green hills and tall palms. This time the fish were more active and aggressive. The small plug caught their attention and I landed a smallish Bluefin Trevally and a two-foot-long needlefish, especially fun because of their visual surface strikes.

After breakfast, my first full meal in two days, Mary and I walked back to the village so that I could meet Maari. The South Seas village looked like a movie set. Scattered around the grassy grounds were simple white wood and bamboo structures of various sizes with thatched palm roofs and few windows. In Fiji they are known as bures. Many were elevated a few feet off the ground. Lush green trees, flowers and sweeping coconut palms spread throughout the village and increased in density further up the hills. A few high clouds gave us some protection from the blazing tropical sun.

Mary introduced me to Maari who was working in her tiny thatched store. We bought dried coconut, pineapple and banana snacks but Maari also had bags of potato chips and Coca Cola for sale. Maari introduced us to two young village men who wore just shorts and sandals. They were friendly and had physiques that would make any athlete jealous; tall with rippling muscles and dark skin glistening in the humidity. Donatello would likely have given an ear to have such models. The locals gave us a brief tour of their village, definitely a highlight of our short stay in Fiji. Mary departed with a hug for Maari and a big red hibiscus flower in her hair.

The following day we flew to Christchurch on the South Island of New Zealand where we picked up our small camper van. I had researched the trout fishing and touring possibilities for months and it was clear that our biggest challenge would be to narrow down our dozens of choices into a fourteen-day journey.

My map was covered with notes. The "must sees" included Mt. Cook, Queenstown, Milford Sound, Lakes Wakatipu and Hawea, Mt. Aspiring National Park and the Franz Josef Glacier. There were at least twenty prime trout fishing rivers and lakes noted in pencil and I hoped to fish at least half of them.

The first major challenge was driving on the left side of the road, British style. I thought I would have it down within a few hours but I was wrong. We made it out of the city without damage but I was mentally exhausted. We had a close call on that first night when the lights of an oncoming vehicle approached on a narrow country road. For a moment I panicked and almost turned the steering wheel right to pass. Whew, that was way too close!

The next morning I pulled out my small roll of white vinyl electrical tape and made an arrow low on the driver's side front window. It pointed to the left towards Mary. This was my guide if I ever had another mental lapse and it definitely reduced the danger and my stress level. I never got comfortable with the three-speed manual tranmission that I shifted with my left hand, but a sloppy shift wasn't dangerous.

Our first fishing stop was at the MacKenzie County Lakes. We drove around for a while taking in the scenery that was similar to eastern Montana with ranches, rivers, forests and snow-covered peaks off in the distance. The Southern Alps that run along the west coast of the South Island squeeze out much of the moisture coming off the Tasman Sea. The results are the glaciers of the West Coast and a drier climate to the east of the mountain spine. Much of the water flowing off the peaks drains to the east creating some of the world's best trout habitat. It was perfect trout water with no trout; not until the 1860s.

Historically, no trout, salmon or char lived in the Southern Hemisphere even though there were hundreds of clean, clear, cold water lakes and rivers. The successful northern salmonid species simply had no way to migrate through the warm equatorial tropics; that is until ingenious Europeans and Americans devised methods to transport fertilized trout eggs alive in cargo ships during the long voyage south. The key was to keep the eggs in moss-insulated wooden ice holds normally used to transport fresh beef and lamb. The first brown trout arrived in New Zealand from European stock previously planted in Tasmania a few years earlier. The first rainbow trout eggs came from the Pacific coast of North America in the 1880s. The trout reproduced and thrived in hundreds of New Zealand's lakes, rivers and streams on both the North and South Islands.

Since there was so much water to cover I decided it would be best to fish, at least initially, where a few locals were fishing. We came to just such a lake where several small fishing boats were out working the water. I had the names and contact information for a few fishing guides but preferred to put my fly fishing experience and research to work. My odds of success would certainly be double or triple with a guide if success were based solely on the number of trout landed. If other factors such as self-reliance and ultimate satisfaction were considered, than the odds would be more difficult to determine.

We had brought two float tubes along from California and that's how I started fishing. While Mary enjoys fly fishing, she is less enthusiastic about the long search preferring just the catching part. She decided to read a book while I tried to find the trout. I geared up with my float tube, waders and fins and headed out on the lake. The rig was basic and one that I had confidence in, a 5-wt. rod, sink tip line and #6 bead head olive woolly bugger.

Under the bright blue sky, I cast, stripped, kicked, cast and stripped zigzagging in and out near the grassy shoreline. Cast, strip, kick, cast, strip, kick, cast, strip, Boom! A nice trout was on! The rod bowed deeply as the heavy trout headed out and down. But I had the benefit of a stout leader and soon had the fish coming my way. A few minutes later it was in the net. My first New Zealand rainbow trout, and a good one at 21 inches. Too beautiful to keep with its scarlet flanks, I carefully removed the hook and sent it on its way back home. That was it for the day but I considered it a success. It wasn't enough action to get Mary out on the water.

As I mentioned, the South Island and its fishing potential reminded me of Montana; the Montana of many years ago. Perhaps it was the limited human population with more sheep than people. The New Zealand waters were rarely crowded with anglers and the ones we met were friendly. A few times we drove onto a private ranch to access a river, always careful to close the gates and respect the land. No one seemed to mind.

At night we stayed wherever we found ourselves, sometimes in organized camping areas but often just out in the country along a scenic lake or river. Our little home on wheels was comfortable and we were never more than an hour or two from a friendly town where we could stop for a meal or restock our food supplies.

Lake Hawea and the Timaru River were high on our list of potential trout hot spots. While most of our New Zealand fishing was blind casting streamer flies, I was determined to walk a few rivers and sight fish in the Kiwi tradition. Mary and I made the long hike while carefully scanning the Timaru River. Near its outlet into the lake, the Timaru dropped through a rocky canyon section with deeper emerald green pools. The slight green tint of the clear water was typical of many rivers we visited, likely due to a small amount of ultra-fine rock flour from the glacial activity upstream. Above the canyon section the small river opened up into a wide valley with sparse forest growth.

I had tied some classic New Zealand dry flies like Greenwell's Glory, and nymphs such as the Hare and Copper and Twilight Beauty at home before our trip. They seemed to be attractor patterns that didn't match a specific insect hatch. I tended to be more confident with the standard Adams, pheasant tails and hare's ears in those situations, flies also popular in New Zealand.

We walked for several hours without spotting a trout in the clear flow. New Zealand trout are known to be low in numbers but often very large, so the search went on. Eventually I spotted a medium-sized trout finning at the head of a short run. There was no visible hatch so I tied on a #14 Adams dry fly. I stayed slightly below and far to the side of the trout and cast above. On the third or fourth drift the trout struck. It was a nice fifteen-inch brown trout. As it turned out, it was the smallest trout of our trip.

We hiked back down to the lake and I headed out in the float tube again. The creek had cut an obvious channel into the lake during low water and I stripped a weighted olive Matuka streamer fly along the deep edges. Eventually, after a few hours of casting, I hooked and netted another 20-plus-inch rainbow. The float tube became an important tool for finding fish in the river outlets and along the lake edges. I was surprised that I didn't see more float tubes given that New Zealanders, from the indigenous Maori in their Waka canoes to the top crews of modern America's Cup super yachts, have always been among the world's best watermen. The Kiwis seem to embrace and master nearly any type of watercraft, but float tubes had not yet become one of them.

We visited Queenstown a few days later, welcomed by the sign that boasted "Adventure Capital of the World". "Anxiety Capital" might be more appropriate if you visit the AJ Hackett Bungy Jump on the nearby Kawarau Bridge. This was the world's first commercial bungy jumping operation and I thought I might give it a try. However, after watching a few terrified but ultimately brave tourists cast their souls off to the mercy of the rubber bands, I decided that I would probably be the one-in-a-million that tangled it around my neck on the way down. Mary had no illusions of taking the 140-foot free fall. I did, however, gather up the courage to try New Zealand's famous lamb with mint jelly that night. Lamb has never been a favorite of mine (read about my experience on the remote Chilean farm and you'll understand) but this wasn't too bad. Mary thought it was among the best she had ever tasted.

Early the next afternoon we visited a Queenstown pub. Two professional club rugby teams were playing on TV and the competing fans' vocal levels were high, encouraged by the tight score and numerous pints of Kiwi beer. We were able to get bits of an introduction to rugby from two friendly locals during short pauses in the action. A few of the fans wore the jersey of the legendary All Blacks, the New Zealand national rugby team known for their extra-tough style of play and pre-game ritual of the Haka, the ancient chant of Maori warriors before going to battle. Many heavily-built and tattooed Maoris, the most southerly of the Polynesian people, have starred on this world-renowned team.

Afterwards we made the long drive along the shoreline of glacier-carved Lake Wakatipu, between the Remarkable Mountain Range and Ben Lomond, through the tiny town of Glenorchy, and finally to the mouth of the Greenstone River. The fishing potential and scenic beauty at the base of the Southern Alps made it a favorite of ours. The Greenstone is known as a top fly-in fishing river but that section was a full day hike or 30-minute helicopter flight above our location at the confluence with Lake Wakatipu.

We took our first short hike along the Greenstone down to the lake armed with a bottle of New Zealand Sauvignon Blanc instead of our fly rods. The rocky knee-deep run in the lower hundred yards of the river and the flow out into the lake looked promising and I planned on getting back at first light. The cool autumn breeze was comfortable but died to a whisper as the evening sun dropped towards the jagged ridgeline. The tranquility was rudely interrupted by the notorious New Zealand sand flies and black gnats so we made a hasty retreat back to the sanctuary of our cozy camper.

I was up before dark the following morning and, after a quick cup of coffee, headed back down towards the lake. There wasn't enough light yet to sight fish the lower river but I did swing my #6 olive/grizzly Matuka streamer through the run for about twenty minutes. Nothing.

The mouth of the Greenstone as it flowed into Lake Wakatipu looked about as good as trout-holding water can; five-to-six-feet deep, sand and fine gravel bottom with some light aquatic vegetation, and a mild current that gradually diminished until it was completely absorbed by the lake about 200 feet out. I began the rhythmic cast and strip of the streamer fly angler.

Fly fishing can take on many personalities and this is one of my favorites. While matching a dry fly hatch usually requires extreme focus, stripping streamers is more of a semi-conscious activity where the repetitive routine of cast, strip, step, cast, strip, step can be almost hypnotic. The angler's mind can wander and ponder without interruption, especially in the pure air of a spectacular mountain setting. Then, the occasional and sudden strike of a heavy fish stimulates a jolt of adrenaline to the blood stream. As many fly anglers know, this often becomes a sort of legal addiction.

The anticipated strike didn't come however, even after an hour. The early morning sun shone on the water as I felt a strange sensation on my boot tops. I looked down at my submerged wading boots to quite a shock. A huge black eel of maybe twenty pounds lay right on top of my wading boots as if it was trying to scratch its belly. This was new to me. I'd seen a few smaller Lamprey eels as a kid but never a freshwater eel of this enormous size. I'd read about the New Zealand longfin eel and knew they had big teeth like their Moray cousins in the sea. Yikes! My feet remained motionless in the thigh-deep water but I continued to cast. Ten minutes later the eel swam off and disappeared back into the lake.

The morning light was strong enough now to revisit the lower river run. This time I had a good opportunity to spot any trout working the water. And there it was, a black shadow waving in the mid-river current. I waded slowly backwards to the bank and then a bit upstream of the fish. The first swing of the streamer was too far in front of the holding trout. I stripped out two feet of line and made another cast. This one looked better. As the Matuka swam down and across, the fish spotted it and made a hard dash towards the fly. Bang! The fish was on, a nice rainbow that immediately jumped high out of the water and then shot back towards the lake. After a quick run down the gravel shoreline, as fast as my clumsy boots and waders would allow, the fish came in right where the river met the lake. Another twenty incher, my only fish that day.

I wondered about the trout of New Zealand, big but often few and far between. My best guess is that it's extremely hazardous to be a small fish there. With all of the big natural lakes in the river systems, any trout that survives to larger size will become an apex predator preying on the supply of smaller baitfish (including small trout) available in the lakes. When those predator trout enter the rivers to spawn or chase insects, any small fish in their path will likely meet its end. The result is a few large brown and rainbow trout that migrate up and down the rivers and into the lakes eating nearly all of the smolts, fingerlings, and even ten-inch trout they encounter. Similar trout ecology exists in the Great Lakes and their tributaries. It might explain why hours of hiking and searching on some of the South Island's most famous trout streams often yielded nothing in my net.

The following morning we drove towards Milford Sound, an iconic New Zealand tourist destination. A storm was moving in from the west and a heavy cloud cover blanketed the sky. The drive through Te Anau and along the Eglinton River could have been in the Swiss Alps with the combination of lush green farmland surrounded by knife-edged peaks. A light rain was falling and some fresh snow was occasionally visible high above us through the fog. The rain fell harder as we boarded our tour boat for the cruise around Milford Sound. The low clouds obscured the view of some of the higher mountains surrounding the deep glacier-carved fjord, but the rain awakened dozens of amazing waterfalls that dropped hundreds of feet down to the sea.

The drifting clouds did allow us a brief view of Mitre Peak, a huge stone pyramid jutting straight out of the ocean; possibly New Zealand's most famous landmark. Mary and I walked out to the bow of the tour boat a few times in our rain jackets to photograph the waterfalls and feel the full force of the storm; a long way from the tropical heat of Fiji. Eventually we became too wet and cold and joined a large group of Japanese tourists standing in line to order sushi below deck.

We visited a pair of smaller lakes the next day just as occasional patches of perfect blue sky began to show through the retreating clouds. A clearly defined snowline ran horizontally a few thousand feet above. As we drove the bank along the head of the lower lake I had to do a double take, and then a triple take. The lake had flooded a few feet over the grassy upper meadow. The water was transparent and the submerged grass was short like it had been recently grazed. Imagine a flooded golf course. Now imagine a flooded golf course with a few dozen huge trout cruising and feeding! It was startling, one of those "once in a lifetime" fishing experience that happen every four or five years if you're on the water enough. Mary didn't need any convincing this time and we were both ready to go twenty minutes later.

We carried our float tubes down to the lakeshore but wanted to wade first. There were at least ten trout in water less than two-feet deep. Slowly and quietly we moved forward trying not to disturb the unsuspecting fish. When we were 40 feet from the first trout Mary made her cast. On the third strip the trout followed and then grabbed her streamer like it hadn't eaten in a month. Fish on! The first long run spooked about half of the shallow-water trout. Mary backed up towards the shore and kept the pressure on. Two shorter runs later the big rainbow laid on its side in a few inches of water; 22 inches! I shot a few photos and then removed the fly.

I was able to get one more sight casting in shallow water, a brown trout just slightly smaller than Mary's, which she proudly announced. By now all of the trout had moved out into deeper water. We switched to the float tubes and landed three more. The largest was 26 inches and I estimated the weight at six or seven pounds; my best New Zealand brown trout. Mary caught a great photo of that fish and my smile before I set it free.

It was our last full day in New Zealand so we packed up and drove back towards Christchurch wishing we had a few more weeks to fish and explore. The photos of those trout and the snow-covered peaks above always bring back great memories. The thought of waking up sick during our flight or driving on the left-hand side of the road...not so much.

11 AL'S PLACE

Everglades, Florida

Wilderness has many faces and countless names around the world. In Florida the name is Everglades, a shallow subtropical river of grass that covers over two-million acres; a 130-mile border between land and sea where beautiful, strange and mysterious creatures swim, slither, soar and crawl.

A while back my wife Mary and I had a chance to explore a portion of the Everglades by canoe. My sister Kris and her husband Keith, Florida residents and experienced flatwater kayakers, invited us for a week-long paddling journey. Kris sent a few books to us in advance so we could familiarize ourselves with canoe travel, Everglades camping and fishing. The Everglades are a world-class sport fishing destination and that locked in my commitment.

Mary and I arrived in Orlando in late September, at least a month ahead of the cooler fall weather. As the four of us departed for Miami and the Everglades, two kayaks on the rack and a canoe in tow, the thermometer read 95 degrees and the humidity was heavy and tropical. We stopped for lunch at a sheik little boardwalk cafe in Miami's South Beach. The waiters, skaters and daters provided quite a flamboyant show of bright color and bare skin. Even our local Southern California beach crowd would have taken notice.

Our final gas station stop in Homestead gave me a good indication of the fishing potential just to the south. The large selection of fishing tackle in the small convenience store surpassed that of many sporting goods stores. Most of the gear was for live bait and lure fishing. There was an interesting combo set-up that I'd never seen before; basically a three-inch red and white floating popper with a ringed eye in the rear instead of a hook. A two-foot leader was tied to the rear eye of the popper and a hook baited with shrimp was tied to the leader end. The popper attracted the fish and the shrimp enticed them to eat. Brilliant! But I'm a fly angler so I was most impressed by the gas station's assortment of artificial flies; Clouser minnows, shrimp patterns, Keys-style tarpon flies, poppers and spoon flies.

An hour later we entered Everglades National Park and stopped at the visitors center to confirm our paddling routes and fill out wilderness permits. The heat and humidity had, no doubt, kept the backcountry crowds down since many of the available permits had not been issued. Due to the temperature and our own inexperience in the

Everglades backcountry, we decided to break our journey into two shorter legs. This would allow us to resupply mid-trip and also to experience two different habitats; one a tidal mangrove swamp and the other a Florida Bay shoreline. Along with the flooded grasslands in view as we drove from the north, these make up the three primary Everglades ecosystems. They are defined by freshwater in the grasslands, brackish in the mangroves and saltwater in the bay.

The southern third of Florida is flat, featureless limestone from ancient coral reefs that tilts southward from giant Lake Okeechobee at an extremely gradual slope of one-twentieth of an inch per mile. Heavy summer rainfall flows south in shallow freshwater seas of grass at a snail's pace of maybe 100 feet per day. Deeper channels, both natural and human-built, crisscross the region.

At locations where the ground elevation rises even a foot above the surrounding land, proper conditions are created for a hardwood hammock, a small island of trees that rarely grow more than twenty or thirty feet tall before being knocked down by ferocious hurricanes. Violent storms both ravage and create the Everglades' ecosystems. Hammocks are home to the Gumbo Limbo tree and the rare Florida Panther.

The freshwater flow from the Everglades, when not intercepted for agriculture, enters Florida Bay, a shallow sea bordered on the east and south by the Florida Keys and on the west by the Gulf of Mexico. The Florida Bay and Keys region is famous and infamous for its eccentric inhabitants, pirates, shrimpers, treasure hunters, fried fish,

Key Lime Pie and tarpon fishing. The bright silver migratory tarpon often exceed a weight of one hundred pounds and are one of the world's greatest sport fish.

An interface zone where fresh and saltwater mix moves seasonally north and south through the southern Everglades depending on the rate of fresh water flowing from the north. Much of the interface zone is comprised of shallow interior tidal flats and mangrove marshes. Fish such as snook, redfish and giant tarpon, normally considered saltwater species, sometimes follow migrating schools of baitfish into the brackish water mixing zone, far up into the mangrove swamps. Locating and hooking these fish is the challenge for Everglades backcountry fly anglers.

Mangroves are nature's tool for gaining back land lost to hurricanes on shallow tropical coastlines. The lush green plants grow densely intertwined in warm tidal saltwater. The portion of the complex root structure between the mud bottom and water's surface provides shelter for fish, shrimp, oysters and myriad other marine creatures. Sediment and dead organic debris build up around the mangrove roots, protected from coastal currents, until tenuous new bits of low-lying land emerge from the sea. The land-building process, which may take hundreds of years, can be wiped out in a few hours as brutal hurricane winds batter the shore. The unique geology and weather patterns in South Florida have created an ecology that is unique in the world. Birds, fish and reptiles abound; the beautiful, the bizarre and the imagined.

The tiny brown and white sign just off the roadway read "Hells Bay". After missing it the first time, we made a U-turn and pulled off onto the shoulder of the road. Above us rose a tangled mass of vegetation about fifteen-feet tall. The thick plant growth was completely impenetrable except for a small tunnel partially filled with black water, an appropriate entry to Hells Bay located ten swampy miles away. As we set the canoe and kayaks on the water, our feet sunk into the thick ooze and the pungent odor of sulfur gas filled the air.

Our gear was similar to what we would carry on a backpacking trip with the added inclusion of two five-gallon water jugs and exclusion of sleeping bags that were replaced with thin bed sheets. Our small tents were critical for refuge from the rain and hoards of mosquitoes. Loading the boats and double-checking our gear took about an hour.

I strung up my 8-wt. fly rod and tied on a gold and white Clouser minnow. We set off with Keith and Kris in their lightweight maneuverable kayaks leading the way while Mary and I followed in the heavily-laden canoe, which we named the "supply barge".

The black tunnel soon entered a small creek of flowing tea-stained freshwater. Fingers of sunlight penetrated the green canopy into the water as a few largemouth bass and bream darted ahead of us. The eight-foot-wide creek followed a sinuous course. Awkward for the first few hours, Mary and I eventually began to gain a little paddling coordination while rounding the sharp bends.

As long as we continued to move, the heat and insects were tolerable. Occasionally we ran face-first into giant spider webs that spanned the entire width of the channel. Kris and Keith in their low-profile kayaks must have slipped underneath. After several hours the twisting narrow creek opened up into a confusing series of mangrove-lined bays. Small plastic poles occasionally marked our route and the exit points from one bay into the next.

Keith paddled ahead and called out each time he located a marker to make sure that our slower canoe wouldn't travel into any dead-end false passageways. It was an incredibly complex maze. A pair of roseate spoonbills, brilliant pink with their diet of shrimp, flew just above the tops of the deep green mangrove forest. We caught a quick glimpse of the Everglade's most famous inhabitant, a six-foot alligator, as it slipped below the water's surface.

Our slow progress in the canoe left us behind schedule as the sun sank low over the endless green horizon. Our goal was the Pearl Bay Chickee but it didn't look like we'd make it before dark; and these confusing waterways were difficult to navigate even in bright sunlight. A check of our charts showed a possible bivouac. The Lard Can campsite was described as the only dry-land wilderness camp in this part of the Everglades. A half hour later our light was nearly gone. The normally convoluted margin of mangrove trees and water became one dull continuous line in the deepening light. I thought about trying to sleep in the floating kayaks and canoe. My conclusion?...... impossible.

Kris took the initiative and darted around the shallow bay in her kayak looking for signs of the campsite. Fifteen minutes later in nearly complete darkness, we heard her, "HEY, OVER HERE!"

Mary and I paddled towards Kris's flashing headlamp far across the water. Ten minutes later our own headlamps caught the tiny "Lard Can" sign hung from a crooked post jammed into the muddy swamp bottom. The needle in a haystack found!

Our elation quickly disappeared, though, when we realized that there was no dry land to be found. Apparently the abnormally heavy summer rains had raised the water level a foot or two above its normal elevation. A sloshing twenty-minute search yielded one small patch of land that rose, at most, one-half inch above the marsh.

We slogged back and forth in the dark through knee-deep water carrying supplies from the canoe and kayaks to our miserable camp. Our sandals sunk into the muck with each sucking step. Mosquitoes and many of their biting cousins emerged in a stinging welcoming committee. Keith sarcastically wondered out loud how this "vacation" might compare with the white sand beaches, palm trees and piña coladas of our Key West trip two years earlier.

Despite our few meager attempts at humor, that night was the most miserable I can remember. The only contender might have been that night years ago when my appendix nearly burst and I was rushed to surgery. The mosquitoes and even more vicious "no seeums" made cooking dinner outside the tents impossible. Just minutes after Mary and

I climbed into our tent and zipped it shut to flee the buzzing mass outside, the nylon floor began to settle into the stinking swamp water. My sheets were soaked from the marsh leaking in and the sweat pouring off my body. The humidity dripped from the tent top above and the thick mangroves surrounding us didn't allow even a puff of breeze into our forlorn camp.

I chuckled just a little. I had actually considered bringing sleeping bags along. I thought about the soldiers that had faced these jungle conditions night-after-night while fighting in WWII and Vietnam. At least no one was shooting at us. I remained wide-eyed all night and jealousy watched Mary sleep. I was so miserable that I never even considered a hungry alligator that could have been in our tent with one quick bite through the thin nylon wall.

The 50-hour night ended at first light. We were back on the water by the time the sun peeked over the mangrove tops. A slight breeze on the open water cooled our skin and kept the biting bugs away. We had plenty of time so I cast and stripped my Clouser minnow from the canoe along the mangrove roots hoping for a strike from a snook or redfish, two of the Everglades top game fish. I couldn't stir any action. We passed our previous night's original destination, the Pearl Bay Chickee.

An easy two-hour paddle in bright sunlight found us at Hells Bay and soon the Hells Bay Chickee. A chickee is a simple yet ingenious home for seeking basic comfort in the hostile Everglade's environment. Originally built by the first human inhabitants of the swamps, the Calusa and Tekesta people, a chickee is a wooden platform elevated about three feet above the water on posts pounded into the muddy bottom. Chickees are built on shallow open water where breezes cool the residents and usually overpower the flight of biting insects. Alligators, in theory, remain safely below.

Our chickee was build of posts and planks (the Calusa used lashed poles) with two twelve-foot-square sleeping platforms connected by a four-foot-wide walkway. A chemical toilet was installed in the center of the walkway. To further enhance this little piece of heaven in Hells Bay, a plywood roof covered each sleeping platform providing protection from the sun and rain.

We tied up the boats and began unpacking our gear. That's when Al made his first appearance. Although we had never met a semi-domesticated alligator, we knew his type. As long-time backpackers in Yosemite and Sequoia National Parks, we were all too familiar with Al's warm-blooded camp-trashing role model; the American black bear. Al emerged from the tangled mangrove roots 50 feet from our chickee. Sinister eyes and nostrils glided just above the inky water's surface, a serpentine wake following behind.

As we learned over the next few days, any commotion on the wooden platforms attracted Al's attention. Apparently free meals from friendly canoeists came easy for Al, but not from us. The Everglades, like all U.S. National Parks, is managed to be as natural as possible while still allowing human visitors. Turkey & cheese casserole was not evolution's idea of a proper alligator's lunch. Al's frequent appearances were comical as often as not. But his jagged overbite and ominous jaws, nearly a third of his six-foot length, reminded us to watch our footing at the edge of the chickee.

The shaded platform proved to be a fine grandstand to view nature's colorful circus. Kris, a tropical bird expert, served as ringmaster introducing us to the cast of osprey, snowy egrets, squawking great blue heron, ibis, and even a bald eagle. Like the eagle's wings, the rhythm of life beats strongly in the Everglades.

Now that we finally had a secure camp, I was able to focus on fishing. I made several canoe trips into the bay to search for fish. Locating promising areas to cast was no problem. Wherever I paddled I found flowing channels, deep mangrove-lined holes, and tidal rips sweeping off lush green points. I cast for hour after hour standing in the wobbly canoe. But the snook, redfish and sea trout were not there.

I paddled in and out of shallow bays and inlets with no distinguishing landmarks. All of the edges were lined with ten-foot-tall mangroves. The thought of becoming lost concerned me. I should have brought a GPS unit along as insurance but had decided that it might dilute the wilderness experience.

Near dark while casting a Florida-favorite gold spoon fly into a grass-lined channel, I finally had a strike. The small fish jumped as I reeled it towards the canoe; an eight-inch largemouth bass. Surprised, I stuck my finger into the water and tasted...fresh! It was rare to have so much fresh water this far to the south. Our experience with the high water at Lard Can should have warned me. I paddled back towards the welcoming light of the lantern on our chickee to find a contented group preparing spaghetti for dinner. We discussed our great day as Al's eyes glowed blood-red out in the bay, following our every move.

As we prepared for bed that night we welcomed the light breeze, until it increased to a squall and drove a brief thunder shower horizontally into our tents. In the darkness, Mary and I woke and spun around to place our bare feet against the collapsing tent wall while lying on our backs. It would have been an amusing sight if there had been any light to see. Fortunately the squall passed quickly and the tent held together. The cool clean water that leaked through was refreshing and we fell into a deep sleep. The following day was as good as the last. During breakfast we all gave the chickee a big "thumbs up", a tiny sanctuary in a hostile but beautiful world.

My streak of poor fishing continued. Even the small baitfish seemed to be gone. But I enjoyed casting, paddling and exploring while more exotic birds flew by or roosted in the tallest mangroves. Mary joined me for a few hours and we watched another osprey glide in slow spirals, also searching for fish.

Apparently the abnormally high summer rainfall and increased freshwater flow from the north had created a temporary fishless zone in the mangrove/bay habitat that is usually brackish or saltwater. The free-roaming salt and brackish water fish that normally frequent this area remained closer to Florida Bay to the south while the freshwater fish were further north. The alligators live in fresh or brackish water while the rarer and larger saltwater crocodiles live in pure saltwater and also overlap with the alligators in brackish water.

For years the Everglades have suffered due to diversions of fresh water flowing south from Lake Okeechobee. Much of the water that historically flowed south into the Everglades is now pumped to farms before it reaches the grasslands. Agricultural pesticides and fertilizers have further degraded the Everglade's ecosystem. The present high-water conditions would leave the Everglades healthier for the near future at least, but had temporarily ruined the fishing. No wonder Al was so hungry.

We departed Hells Bay the following day. Mary and I paddled with more skill picked up over the previous few days. With long strokes and a lighter canoe, we reached the car in under five hours. I made a few casts into promising water and kept my abysmal streak going. After unloading the boats and storing them on the rack and trailer, we drove south to road's end and Flamingo, the National Park Headquarters along the edge of Florida Bay. We spent a day in luxury with air conditioning, cold drinks, lobster and bug-less sleep at the old Flamingo Lodge.

The next paddling leg of our journey would take us along the Florida Bay shoreline west to Clubhouse Beach. We liked the sound of that. I expected much better fishing. By the time we were restocked and packed, it was nearly 2 PM as our tiny flotilla emerged from the Flamingo Marina. This time the water teamed with life. Swirls, ripples and splashes accompanied us for hours. Occasionally a huge tarpon would roll, its foot-wide back arching above the water's surface like a sea serpent. I tried a few casts but an earlier gale had broken loose thousands of floating grass and seaweed strips, which immediately fouled my fly.

We reached Clubhouse Beach in late afternoon....and were immediately reminded of Florida's reputation for practical jokers. We didn't expect a real clubhouse but we did expect a real beach. How wrong we were. The shoreline was slick, steep mudstone with no sand. It was backed up by four-foot piles of rotting seaweed with a swamp on the other side.

As darkness approached, the wind disappeared, the humidity soared and thousands of vicious biting insects went on patrol. We attempted to shovel the tall stacks of seaweed with our paddles to clear spaces for the tents. It sent swarms of hypodermic-nosed sand flies into a rage. A large creature thrashed on the surface of the shallow bay only fifty yards out. I had read about the big hammerhead and bull sharks that fed here in low light. Dozens of fireflies flashed out in the swamp as the intense heat and biting insects became too much to bear. "I would rather paddle all night than take anymore of this!" I shouted out.

There were no arguments. Ten minutes later we were back on the dark water with the sharks, headed on a long journey back to Flamingo. The rhythm of the paddling, the darkness, and our fatigue combined to put us into a hazy mental state. Thousands of brilliant stars overhead were nearly outdone by flashing comets underwater. Lime green trails of phosphorescent algae glowed in ten-foot streaks as mullet fled the approaching canoe.

As the tide ebbed, Mary and I were forced a few hundred yards offshore to maintain sufficient depth for the loaded canoe. Keith and Kris cruised in six-inch-deep water along the shoreline, flashing their headlamps occasionally in our direction to maintain silent contact. The sound of the sea grass tips along the canoe bottom made a subtle hiss. Our dreamy rhythm was suddenly interrupted by a hard THUD! The canoe shuttered as the water erupted right at the bow. Five seconds later it was quiet. I can only imagine that we had struck a sleeping shark, tarpon or crocodile.

The spectacular night voyage ended successfully at Flamingo around midnight. We woke up the lodge's night manager and fell asleep in soft beds feeling good about our decision to flee the ironically-named Clubhouse Beach. It has forever remained a joke among the four of us.

After a few hours of sleep I woke at 5 AM to begin rigging my rods. I needed to explore last night's water in the daylight. My 8-wt. fly rod seemed tiny for taking on some of the huge fish I had seen, or thought I had seen, the previous day. So, along with my fly rod, I packed a heavier spinning rod rigged with 18-lb. monofilament line. I'm a pure fly angler in freshwater but occasionally resort to less artistic and more powerful methods in the salt. Sometimes, with minimal guilt, I'll use a reel with more gears and moving parts. After all, I tell myself, I'm an engineer in my other life.

The rest of our group let me know that I was on my own. They declared their Everglade's experience complete and went back to sleep. I walked out the door and dragged the canoe across the lawn and down to the water's edge. Just prior to shoving off I decided to run back and grab my camera, the waterproof one Mary had bought for me after I ruined several cheaper models on fishing and sailing trips.

I retraced the previous day's (and night's) course paddling for about 30 minutes until I reached Bradley Key, a small mangrove island three or four hundred yards from shore. My Everglades fishing book described a hundred-year-old hole here that had been dredged out to create an anchorage for commercial shrimp and fishing boats. I found it by plunging my canoe paddle into the water until I could not feel the bottom mud. The hole was a good five-minute paddle across and I fished every part of it. The water was flat calm but the clarity was not good, about eighteen inches, due to the previous morning's wind.

After several hours of casting, I hooked and released a nice four-pound snook on a gold spoon fly; my first real Everglades fish catching experience. I was satisfied that I had done it on my own but also convinced that a few days of guided fishing would be a good way to accelerate my learning curve in such a huge and complex fishery. I now considered my own Everglades experience complete and prepared to return to the group. That's when I saw the first monstrous silver back roll in the dredge hole. The tide had receded to the point where the hole, about 100-yards wide, was now clearly defined by the shallow sea grass-filled water surrounding it. Another massive tarpon rolled.

Remember that gas station in Homestead with the huge selection of fishing tackle for sale? My fishing book had recommended a lure called the Bagley's Finger Mullet, "tarpon magic" wrote the author. I had purchased a five-inch-long tan model. Hands shaking, I dug it out of my tackle bag and tied it to the spinning rod with a few feet of 60-pound shock tippet.

Standing in the canoe, I cast and retrieved, cast and retrieved, cast and retrieved. Five minutes later the lure came to a cold stop twenty-feet out; no movement. I'd snagged the bottom most likely. Then the line began to rise to the surface with powerful intent. The next few seconds are clearly and permanently imprinted on my memory. In thousands of great fishing moments, this would be the most amazing.

The silver rocket, nearly seven-feet long, exploded through the surface and hung in the spray of a thousand water drops above my eyes. The tarpon flipped several times in mid-air before striking the water hard and sending a wave towards the canoe. Fearful of swamping, I immediately went to my knees while straining to keep a one-handed grip on the rod. Once back in the water, the huge fish swam rapidly away as my reel whined.

Without enough drag to slow the surge, I figured the excitement would be over soon. But when the tarpon reached the grass-lined flats encircling the dredge hole about 200 feet away, it stopped unwillingly to swim into the shallow water. I had a chance! I reached over with my right hand to start the timer on my watch.

As the one-sided battle continued, I couldn't put enough pressure on the line to move the tarpon much. But the tension was enough to pull the canoe towards the fish. The angry tarpon made another acrobatic leap, ran out a hundred feet and then made another. Each time I was amazed by its massive size.

I knew that accounts of this fish would be hard to believe, so I reached into the tackle bag with my left hand and pulled out the camera during a brief moment while the tarpon sulked. I snapped many photos during the battle even though I lost what small semblance of control I had over the fish each time. I caught the glimmering mass in mid air several times. The head and open mouth were as big as a five-gallon bucket!

As the battle wore on for over an hour, I wondered how it would end. I had no chance of pulling the monster into the canoe and didn't want to. It was a spectacular monster that I wanted to release in good shape after experiencing all of its power and determination. As the tarpon tired it came alongside the canoe and towed me slowly around the dredge hole. Every few minutes it surfaced near me and gasped for air, a characteristic that allows tarpon to temporarily survive in dirty water with low dissolved oxygen.

Many times I brought the great fish within a few feet of the canoe. It was huge, nearly half the length of the boat. The scales were the color and size of bright silver dollars. Each time the tarpon neared I kneeled on the bottom of the canoe worried that it might be capsized with the next surge of that big tail. The rod bent into a deep inverted U. I reached for the lure near the corner of the huge mouth but each time the powerful fish pulled away. The lure looked small in the massive jaws but I wanted to get it out before the tarpon and I parted ways.

Several hours into the fight, I noticed a red mark forming on the edge of the tarpon's lower jaw; apparently some bleeding where the hooks held in the cavernous mouth. That was it. I checked my watch. The battle had ensued for two hours and fifteen minutes and we had a flight to catch out of Miami later that afternoon. I grabbed the leader and pulled hard. The tattered monofilament parted near the lure.

The giant tarpon swam away near the surface gaining speed as it sensed its freedom. I turned the canoe towards Flamingo and headed in feeling a bit stunned. Wow.

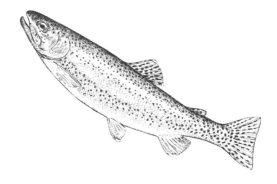

12 FLY FISHING FOR NEWBIES

if you have a passion for travel and adventure, you can enjoy the stories in these pages whether you are a fly angler or not. Nevertheless, for non-fly anglers a brief description may be useful and might even convince you to give fly fishing a try.

Fly fishing differs from other types of sport fishing in several ways. The fly angler casts an artificial "fly" comprised of various combinations of feathers, fur, yarn, tinsels, beads, wire, synthetic and all sorts of decorative materials tied to a fishhook. Flies were originally tied to imitate the insects that the target fish were eating. But today, the term "fly' when referring to fly fishing can be an imitation of nearly any fish food including baitfish, shrimp, fish eggs, frogs, worms, snails, crabs and others in addition to insects which include adults, larvae and pupae. Many flies are just bright "attractor patterns" that do not imitate anything in nature, but may stimulate a fish's curiosity or territorial instincts. Since fish don't have hands, my theory is that they will often grab and inspect an object with their mouths. Flies are categorized as "dry flies" that float on the water's surface, "wet flies" that are smaller flies fished sub-surface to imitate a swimming insect or small baitfish, "streamers" that are larger flies fished subsurface to imitate baitfish, and "nymphs" that are fished subsurface to imitate immature aquatic insect stages.

Unlike other types of sport fishing, a fly rod flexes during the cast due to the weight of the fly line. Spinning and casting rods are different because they use a heavy lure or weight at the end of the line to flex and load the rod during the cast. Fly lines come in different "weights", different thicknesses that match the stiffness and strength of the fly rod, the lightest lines for small trout and panfish and the heaviest lines for large saltwater fish such as tarpon and even tuna, sharks and marlin up to 150 pounds and more.

Fly reels hold the fly line and come in various sizes to match the weight and thickness of the line. Besides the fly line, fly reels are spooled with additional "backing", thin strong line that is attached to the back end of the fly line allowing a strong fish to run out more than the 100-foot length of the typical fly line. Fly reels usually have an adjustable drag to slow the hooked fish down without breaking the short clear section of nylon monofilament or fluorocarbon leader material that connects the fly to the fly line.

Fly line and rod weights (wt.):

0 to 3-wt.	small trout and pan fish
4-wt.	light trout
5-wt.	standard trout
6 to 7-wt.	medium heavy trout and light bass
8-wt.	light salmon, standard bass, steelhead and bonefish
9 to 10-wt.	standard salmon, medium saltwater for snook and permit
11 to 13-wt.	heavy saltwater for tarpon, sailfish and smaller tuna
14 to 16-wt.	extra heavy saltwater for tuna, marlin and sharks

Most fly rods are around nine feet in length although specialty rods may be as short as six feet and as long as fifteen feet. Different types of fly lines are available in each weight; some float on the water's surface while others sink at various rates depending on the depth that the angler wants to fish the fly.

Modern fly anglers are often conservationists and frequently practice catch-and-release fishing. Flies are rarely taken deep into the mouth of a fish and are, therefore, easy to remove with minimal harm to the fish. Fly fishers are able to enjoy the challenge and excitement of fishing while releasing their catch to live on whenever they choose. This practice has encouraged "zero limit, catch-and-release" regulations in many waters in the U.S. and around the world. As the late great fly fisherman Lee

Wulff once said, "A fish is too valuable to catch just once." That does not mean that there isn't controversy in fisheries management styles and the opinions of each individual fly angler.

Efforts to preserve natural aquatic habitats and support native human populations around the world account for the ever-growing number of lodge owners and adventurous fly anglers that have joined the trend of "ecotourism". Ecotourism encourages tourists to visit wild places around the world with minimal environmental impact, while bringing economic benefit to the indigenous people who serve as guides and lodge staff. Good examples can be found in Mongolia, the Amazon basin, Pacific Islands and other worldwide locations.

A few popular fly rod sport fish that are discussed in these pages include:

Steelhead, rainbow trout that live most of their adult lives in the ocean and spawn in freshwater rivers like their close relatives the salmon. Steelhead are among the most prized of all fly fishing species and can grow to 40 pounds, although a twenty-pound fish is a prize. Steelhead are know for their spectacular runs and leaps when hooked and have inspired some of the most beautiful and colorful attractor fly patterns. They are native to the Pacific drainages of British Columbia, southeastern Alaska, eastern Russia, California, Oregon and Washington. Rainbow trout transplanted to the Great Lakes often grow to immense size and migrate up lake tributaries to spawn during winter and spring. Although not of ocean origin, these huge rainbows are a great fly rod fish and many also call these fish steelhead. Steelhead runs in their native rivers have been reduced dramatically over the past 50 years due to excessive commercial gill netting in the river mouths, human degradation of river spawning habitat, dams, ocean net pen farming of Atlantic salmon that degrades water quality and increases parasites, and warming ocean waters. Fly anglers are among the most ardent conservationists seeking answers to reverse the trend of decreasing steelhead stocks.

Bonefish, a smaller silver fish found in the most beautiful tropical waters on earth. Know as the "ghost of the flats", speedy bonefish move in and out of shallow water with the tides and are often stalked on foot while "sight" fishing. As the name implies, sight fishing involves searching and casting to fish that have been spotted in the water as opposed to "blind" casting where the angler casts into likely looking water without seeing the fish that are hopefully below the water's surface. Bonefish are typically two-to-ten pounds although huge models of up to twenty pounds are sometimes seen (but rarely caught by fly anglers) in warm shallow Pacific waters including Hawaii. Pound-for-pound, no fish can accelerate like a bonefish. Their lightning runs across the shallow tropical flats when hooked make them among the most exciting fly rod fish and create an extreme contrast for the sight-fishing angler that quietly stalks bonefish like a heron.

Tarpon, a large silver migratory fish found in sub-tropical coastal waters on both sides of the Atlantic Ocean including Florida, Africa, and Mexico. Famous for their acrobatic jumps, tarpon can grow to 200 pounds and 100-

pound fish are common putting them among the greatest of all fly rod sport fish.

Sea trout, a sea-run brown trout that, like steelhead and salmon, lives out most of its adult life in the ocean but returns to its birth river to spawn. Juvenile sea trout live in fresh water (like resident freshwater brown trout that are genetically identical) but then migrate out to sea where they grow quickly. The scientific name for the life cycle of sea-run trout and salmon is "anadromous". The world's largest sea trout are transplants from Europe to the island of Tierra del Fuego in southern Patagonia (Argentina and Chile) where they can grow in the South Atlantic Ocean to 40 pounds before they return to freshwater rivers to spawn.

Atlantic salmon, the king of riverine fly fishing species (although this is argued by many steelhead fishermen). Atlantic salmon can grow to over 50 pounds but a 30-pound fish is a trophy today. Atlantic salmon are the only native salmon in the Atlantic Ocean and are found in the rivers of Ireland, Great Britain, Scandinavia, Russia (Arctic Ocean drainage), Finland, Iceland and eastern Canada. Atlantic salmon are credited with inspiring modern fly fishing in Scotland and England starting several hundred years ago. Traditional Atlantic salmon flies are colorful works of art that often contain plumage from some of the world's most exotic birds. Today, some of these birds have become scarce and are illegal to hunt. In response, some of the more valuable bird species are now raised on farms for their feathers. Atlantic salmon runs in their native rivers have been reduced dramatically over the past 50 years due to excessive commercial fishing in the ocean, human degradation of river spawning habitat, ocean net pen farming of Atlantic salmon that degrades water quality and increases parasites, and warming ocean waters. Fly anglers are among the most ardent conservationists seeking answers to reverse the trend of decreasing salmon stocks.

Arctic Grayling, a beautiful fish common to Alaska is known for its large iridescent lavender dorsal fin somewhat resembling a miniature sailfish. The Arctic grayling is a salmonid related to trout and are typically ten-to-twenty-inches long. Arctic grayling are a great fly rod species found in some of the world's most remote northern waters.

Trevally, heavily-built apex predators found on tropical reefs in the Pacific and Indian Oceans. Trevally are in the jack family and there are many species. The most popular for fly anglers are the smaller Bluefin and Golden Trevally (five-to-twenty pounds) and the Giant Trevally, thugs of the reef that can reach 100-plus pounds and are considered one of the top prizes in all of fly fishing.

Back Cover Photos clockwise from upper left:

Preparing our inflatable jet boat "Delfin" for an exploration of the remote Rio Tic Toc in Patagonia with La Guiteca crewman Señior Soto standing by

Sea-run brown trout in Iceland

Brown bear (grizzly) paw prints near our tent in Alaska

Learning the Polynesian sport of Patia Fa, spear throwing at a coconut target with the local villagers on remote Anaa Atoll

Preparing for another flight into the Alaskan bush

Late evening barracuda on Anaa Atoll in French Polynesia

Made in the USA
Las Vegas, NV
21 October 2021

32761721R00114